Against the Current

First published in the United Kingdom in 2023 by
The Choir Press

ISBN 978-1-78963-383-2

Against the Current

What's Going On?

0:1

This is a story of a young adult male who grew up in an urban metropolis on the south coast of Britain. I was born two years before the beginning of the twenty-first century, and the years of my childhood development would be accompanied by lightning-speed advances in interactive media and communication technology. My generation was the first to have smartphones at the turn of our teens. Since then, these handheld devices, in which whole lives are organised, have become central to many people's definition of technology. Suddenly, there were people at my school spending more time, and doing more things, on social media: aka 'the socials'. The socials were taking up a bigger role in my life as a schoolboy, because people in my age group were sharing stories and gathering information through clouds of data compacted into devices small enough to fit in their pockets. This was the start line, for a race about to be run.

I, like so many others, would struggle to cope with the socials as they became more significant throughout my time in secondary school. I was a very sensitive child, and I always felt two steps behind my friends in adopting technology into my life. It meant that my understanding of the socials was always on their terms, not mine, so that the way I used them was always an attempt to replicate theirs. I might have been a very sociable individual, but this aim was impossible to achieve. I wanted to fit in and be somebody, but the obvious path of always being up to date with the changing flavours of the socials was, deep down, neither something I wanted nor what I needed, really. It just felt exciting and full of opportunity! I strongly believed that this was the single best way to find my feet in the world around me. My self-esteem and a sense of place would be secure forever if I satisfied the next impulse to engage with an online interaction in response to all the activity in this one world.

Besides the natural teenage social habits, my instinctive desire to be connected by any means necessary pulled my mind into a wormhole of distraction and visual obsessiveness, which the socials stretched to an uncomfortable length. I felt incomplete and then diverted from all the things I loved doing. I was totally unaware of the hazards associated with it all, a measurement of success amongst my peers that I wanted but couldn't excel in. Expectations from the people I connected with were an unhealthy influence on mine. This norm and my reaction to it would lead me to fall into personal tragedy and furthermore change the rest of my life. It would lead to the deterioration of my mental wellbeing to the point where I was facing death all on my own.

Fortunately, after a lot of work and unconditional love and support from my friends and family, my mind has reached a far healthier balance. But it has also meant that I've had to create an 'alternative lifestyle' from my extreme position in relation to the technological turn in my surrounding environment. The current has swept me away from the closest shore, but thankfully I land on another, after being lost at sea for so long. Now I'm on a shore with a different view of the ocean.

0:2

The real things in life were running away from me. I closed my mind off from trying new activities and properly engaging with people at an age when it was crucial to my development. I said no to things that I could have done, vouching for the easier option of living more of my life online. This was coupled with the shared space in school, which gave the socials a much stronger grip on me. In my head it was social, but my way of trying to make friends followed by my desire to connect had swept me away from reaching my potential in a variety of pursuits, like competitive sport or school grades. What made me more vulnerable was that the ones caring for me had no idea about the extent of the socials' damaging effects. It was all new. Me and all the other kids were on the front line without any effective protection or guidance from the adults. I mean, how could the adults have known? Firstly, the impacts of the socials on mental health were never going to be a conversation started by me. I only cared about its propensity to entertain or make me seem cool. Secondly, my actual use of social media was largely private. My parents knew what platforms I had but they didn't see what I was up to on them. They didn't see that when I was bored, I would see photos of people I barely knew having fun together, and then feel lonely and totally inadequate. There was no genuine insight into my personal relationship with the socials, while some content and interactions were seriously touching a lot of deeper feelings. I didn't have as much fun as intended. There was no education about how to use it safely, as lessons at school would barely scratch the surface. The closest to it I remember were lessons about cyberbullying in IT classes, or PSHE lessons (personal, social, and health education) about healthy living more generally. It was great to hear from a younger relative recently that he'd received lessons in e-safety that include the topic of mental health because I really could have done with that when I was at school. I really could have done with understanding the connection between the socials and conditions such as depression or anxiety. Even the smallest glimpse into how the mind's complicated state was affected by how I used the socials would have made me take more care. I wasn't even thinking about how much time I should be spending on them, rather having my attention focused on being in the loop and involved in something which, paradoxically, took me away from a much brighter course.

I was under the impression that everyone around me was doing just fine while spending a lot of time on the socials. Some people probably were, but there wasn't a clear picture here. I assumed, no matter how down and preoccupied I was, that my issues were not being intensified and further ingrained by my use of the socials. I'd developed a relationship that would make me want to minimise my time online as much as possible. Therefore, I'd grown to prefer any in-person interaction to a virtual one, even if it took more time and energy. But this was an outcome after I associated it with every negative emotion as a troubled teen rather than a philosophy in my mind. I was torn for years after school had finished about how I would engage with the online world since personal health and 'staying connected' had begun to feel like separate aims. And there is so much pressure nearly everywhere I go to participate to the point where my identity can be in disorder. I am told again and again the reasons to live more of my life online, although the benefits that people have had do not relate to my own experience. Despite all the difficulties I face when moving against the current, I haven't given up in trying to stay afloat above the hazards from staying away from the closest shore. But the current is stronger than I anticipated, so I must work hard to find safety away from this shore.

Part I

1:1

"I've got one hundred friends on Facebook now!" a year 7 classmate said to me.

I didn't really comment, having no interest in this proud exclamation. It was just some online thing I'd only heard about. At the time, it was only on people's desktops at home, although I did seem to think that the person boasting about this goal was a member of something which had won them popularity. But I hadn't yet understood what people did on social media. What they did as in who they wanted to be, and which people they were showing their association with. It wasn't in my face consistently enough in my early secondary school years to make me see it as an integral part of society. It wasn't yet powerful enough.

Appealing to me much more as a young boy were the action-packed games consoles. Graphic and stimulating, playing video games was a much cooler pastime than trading cards. Very often after school, I would be shooting up bad guys at a friend's house. It was an enormously fun escape route, because I was neither able to purchase these games at the shop nor have my parents give them to me. I also didn't have any older siblings, so my enjoyment of this thrilling form of entertainment was always a branch of my social life, despite it involving me being sat in a dimmed room staring at screens for hours. I had my own devices at home, but it was never the ones my mates were chatting enthusiastically about. I wouldn't really get my hands on a fashionable, top-grossing machine until later in my teens. By then they were all synchronised together into an online realm as phones had the power to receive data and serve the same functions as a touch-screen mp3 player. There was a sense that a circle of respectable membership had been constructed as the talk on the school bus was frequently the latest feature from these platforms. Every time, I quietly listened. It was the topic that brought excitement, endlessly chatted about while it was often literally in their hands. I tried to hide my far inferior gadgets. Life was starting to look dull if I wasn't a part of this. Since that was the talk, and I wasn't a member, it got quite lonely at times. Every day, I slowly believed that I was worth less than the people sitting around me. The only way to improve was to set my feet ready to keep up with their pace. It was on my mind so much that I began to devalue some of the important things in life, like education or heathy living. I wanted to be a member.

The standard was set. Of course, there were the shoes you had to wear, but that wasn't prioritised like the security of belonging in the race. Because that was how you gained supporters. That deep concept of friendship acted out as mates were made through consuming these hook-laden blocks of digital fun. I might have played football matches, but my attention was more focused on taking part in this growing area of engagement because that was how I thought I was going to be a better person in the eyes of everyone I talked to. As more classmates were talking to me, there was a feeling of a magnetic pull towards a growing virtual space that the minds of my friends were following.

After being asked if I had Facebook, the person sat next to me in maths was teasing me by telling the girl that, "He doesn't have Facebook, because he doesn't have a life."

The online features of the games my friends were playing had become the most popular part of the experience too. As I watched my mate defend a house with his team against a horde of zombies, I felt a strong desire to think of a method of persuading my parents to buy me this stuff.

"You should get it!" I'd hear around me at break time, "Then you can add me on it. This is my online name."

I'd played online computer games before, but this was something else. I was about to spread my wings and fly with all the other birds who had come of age to explore the world without the supervision of their parents. And this was a fresh part of the world that I got to fully take in with my senses, without its potential hazards being known to anyone. Feeling my identity being strung together as I grew, I wanted more of this, so that I could exceed my state of being alone and small. Nothing else mattered to me.

1:2

Different members of my family reminisce about my free-spirited attitude when I was a very young child.

My grandfather once told my seventeen-year-old self that, "You didn't even think about it. You just did it."

I became far less capable of losing myself in the moment. Becoming a teenager naturally involved me trying to see my appearance in the eyes of my peer group and thinking that every movement was being closely judged by other people.

It felt like I had very strict parents compared to all my friends. There was a lot of bickering at home because I saw everyone at school appearing to have more freedom in choosing what stuff to own so that they could follow any fashion and afford to have less discipline in using things without getting nagged by their folks. For example, besides my countless attempts at trying to persuade Mum to allow me a TV for my bedroom, she wouldn't budge until I was sixteen.

Before then I'd be met with, "No, darling."

"But Mum, please!" I protested. I wasn't getting anywhere past this wall.

"I said no."

"Everyone else has one!" I tried every angle of reasoning.

"No, I'm not letting you have a TV in your room, Luke. It's not good for you."

"Why not?"

"Because I said so." My desperation in this age-old argument wouldn't have existed if it wasn't for the terms for connection in school. We had to share experiences around the fruits of this colourful technological revolution. Despite my stable upbringing, I falsely believed that my parents were bad people, because I couldn't access the normal way of fitting in with the kids I hung around with. I wanted a TV in my bedroom so I could game online with them and belong. I wouldn't be bothered about being spoilt in this way if it wasn't for how modern technology was distributed to children without any foresight into what it could be doing to our mental health.

"Where were you last night, Luke? Everyone was online." I tried my best to brush the question aside every week. It was never an option to tell my circle of gamer mates that I wasn't allowed to play games later in the evening while my parents watched TV.

This would eventually be a factor in my social exclusion as someone told me that, "You're on at the deadest time. Everyone goes on later." For the rest of the school break, this person wouldn't interact with me, preferring to turn to the huddle that laughed and enthusiastically reflected on the group's session the day before. Many would receive this kind of comment and behaviour behind the childish boundary to belonging, but it hit me hard because of its consistency and questioning of a delicate individuality.

"What do you do at that time?" they asked, while referring to their peak online time in the lobby. Sometimes, I couldn't think of a defence, and it could cut deeper because it played into this intense race for worth in the eyes of my generation. Following these verbal attacks. I would think about it at home after school, and focus a lot of time and energy into progressing in the latest edition of popular online games by achieving a higher level and unlocking the most powerful tools. I was compensating.

My interest in performing perfectly in the online gaming world transferred over to watching videos on YouTube. I would subscribe to channels typically featuring young adult males recording their gameplay with voiceovers about the very intricate details that would help you get an edge over other players. Coupled with the social element with school friends, editors producing content from their set-ups would gain a fast-growing following as videos were uploaded of them mastering the latest games with their skill and knowledge. We all wanted a superior advantage. From the ages of thirteen to sixteen, it captured my imagination. Any euphoria I had from being seen to win these games that were on people's radar gave me more determination to follow this new wave of entertainment idols. Since the social pastime became significant for fitting in, I wanted to be as good as these top gamers and talk about the games like them. I therefore wanted to be them. Unfortunately, I was still a schoolchild, who was now heavily distracted from the responsibility of that position.

What was important about online gaming for the purpose of attaching my life to the socials was that there was a huge crossover between the different platforms in sharing experiences and gathering information. The recording of a gaming session, for viewers online, contributed to the development of a title now known as an influencer. An influencer has an especially large number of followers, so they therefore influence the trends. Gamers, as well as many other vloggers who began their careers from the bedroom, grew in popularity amongst anyone engaged in online activity. The consumption of their videos signalled the rise of a new generation of internet sensations who would eventually become labelled as celebrities. Like gaming, activities ranging from comedy to make-up tutorials or vlogging day-to-day life gathered more views at an exponential rate. They were becoming the new rock stars. Whatever they did online could be found out on multiple sites, and countless children have tried to emulate it. YouTubers mattered a lot, and there I was being told by my mate to get a smartphone or a TV for my room. That was the path to becoming a member. Couldn't I just be content to be without?

There were more factors pressing on me to aspire to be anyone but myself throughout the different stages of online transformation. The YouTuber became a figure that added more appeal to spending time online through its social features, opening a door to peer into where people found their success. It took over my view on the best way to make friends as I began to care a lot more about popularity. I felt I had to go down that route or else be no one at all, someone separate from a whole community of fun.

1:3

I downloaded Facebook at the age of thirteen, which was relatively late for my peer group at the time. I didn't feel much of a buzz from setting it up, despite some of the light pressure from a wide array of different personalities. It was Dad who facilitated it. He was using it as a casual network to keep in touch with friends and family all over the globe.

This was my first proper introduction to an official social media site, and I was unaware of how my school friends were behaving on it, even if I heard about it in conversation. Soon after adding friends, I posted messages on people's walls that were a bit odd, failing to realise that everyone befriended by me or them could see it all on their newsfeed. One time, I received a message from a classmate making fun of me for posting a list of nicknames on a friend's wall and I was in shock.

Another early mystery to me was when people who I'd never spoken to in my year group were sending me friend requests. I slowly found that knowing little more than someone's name and usual circle of friends made it acceptable to connect on the site where identities were explored. The process was interesting to everyone. They wanted to see a picture of other people's lives in the same bracket as them, to compare and see how they presented us. Who were we associating with? Was my social life as successful as theirs? How many friends did I have? My first two years on Facebook were managed through my touchscreen mp3 player, but that was utilised more for music and games than the socials. By my fifteenth birthday, I was on a tablet, on which I checked Facebook every day.

My initial relationship with Facebook was healthy, although it did implant the idea that the quantities displayed on it represented worth. The number of friends on a list, or the number of likes on a post (especially the profile picture). I began to worry about it because it felt like it was becoming a more significant measure of how good your life was, and you knew everyone could see it. There was also a twist when you had people on your friend list who you hadn't spoken to for years, acting to rekindle nothing more than seeing the figures on their profiles. It felt almost competitive, like leaving one sports team for another, and wanting to be seen to be excelling there in front of your former teammates as a show of a good move. Even if you consider whether it's a genuine picture of people's lives, it can still influence your perspective on yourself. It made me feel like I wasn't interesting to other people. Having things with friends to bond over didn't change that. Going through puberty at the same time, my sense of being was far from settled, while my scrolling on the socials cemented how I was seeing myself. I wasn't ready for all these things at once. The building was unstable; its structure didn't develop in an order that was right. My eyes were on everyone else's posts, their design blueprinted as a template for my own. It was uncomfortable because I was different, but this assessment made me feel like I had to mimic another design for life. The technology was so fast. My attention followed the kids in my classes, because getting closer to them was prioritised over anything. I believed that the more I could connect, the bigger I'd be. The outcomes had left my control before my young mind could register them. It was an invasion, and I surrendered under the impression that better things would come afterward, a greatness achieved, an identity secured. It all looked better on the other side.

The summer after finishing secondary school, around 300 out of 360 of my year group had me as a friend on Facebook. The majority I'd say had no sentimental connection to me, but they could see pictures of me and what attention I would gather. I thought deeply about the profiles I saw, ignoring the limits of their resemblance to the people who posted them. Responding to it was an investment without knowing anything about many of the lives behind the images they presented. It was an evaluative exercise that gave a euphoric feeling upon the consumption of the newsfeed that was becoming a priority, despite the way it affected how I felt about myself. I kept on scrolling, and I didn't feel good about it once I put it down. But then when I didn't feel good, I scrolled again. The ways it functioned kept growing. The effect it had on influencing how I valued myself: my body, my friends, my possessions, came before I understood how superficial their sources were.

1:4

The classroom could become a minefield at times. You would speak out loud and answer questions from the teacher, thinking in the back of your mind that if you were to say something embarrassing, it would be seized upon by a class clown looking for material to make the popular people laugh at your expense. This sounds like a familiar occurrence in school life, but what really magnified the social anxiety behind it was that you knew it could trickle into some running joke that would be echoed on the socials for your list of 'friends' to see. It could also work the other way round. Saying something on the socials could come back to bite you at school when someone would bring it up in front of a crowd looking for entertainment. I once completely misinterpreted a post and commented on it for all to see, so confident that I had made an impact that was funny. About an hour later, I looked at my tablet to see that someone had completely roasted me for missing the point, generating likes from the members of different gangs at school. It only took one person bringing it up the next day to confirm the humiliation, knocking my confidence online for the next month. I remember praying that some other poor kid would become the new laughing stock, as my face went red from the howls all around me. It was a huge relief when something worse happened to someone a couple of days later to shift the attention. Once I saw that, I deleted my comment when it became old news. No one received a notification from deleted comments so no one could remind themselves by looking back on the comment section of the post. The atmosphere remained, however. I had to keep up with the advances in the socials to prevent my embarrassment again.

I began to feel unsafe in school, but not because I could have been verbally abused or beaten up. The way I saw myself could be altered in seconds by a series of actions behind the scenes that the teachers could hardly pick up on. Every little thing could be judged from one shallow engagement. My own judgement was clouded and I couldn't consistently engage in any learning. A long-term disorder was created by this high maintenance dynamic, throwing off any level-headed decision-making while my focus was on maintaining an image to prevent myself from feeling inadequate.

By the time I was halfway through secondary school, it was becoming common for people my age to carry a smartphone. At fourteen, I saw a phone and computer fused together, an oblong that could receive clouds of data in public without always needing a Wi-Fi router for the connection. I wouldn't get one until two years later, but I felt its looming presence. It was there to be fed, and each single unit could present a spectacle of the posts of others that determined what was interesting within the social world to be accessed in a click of a button. Everyone was naturally looking over their shoulders, but now the lens could be shared by anyone connected to the observer. At school, conformity was the way to achieve a higher rank as an adequate online member to be an adequate person all around. I was becoming more like who my schoolmates wanted me to be, and the result was inauthentic to say the least. The distance was close between the users, but my idea of success looked to mirror whoever I saw online rather than being myself. The newsfeed changed how I wanted to look, and personal self-expression became more difficult amongst anyone I saw on there. It could connect all the worst teen behaviours like the bravado found in exposing someone for doing it differently. It got complicated, but the symbolic friend request slipped me in, young and very inexperienced with the technology.

School politics could be harsh and difficult to influence. The online activity could change how I felt towards someone the next day, and where I was once behind the convoy of members, now I was in the thick of them. An arena was set. Inside it, the quality of friendships could be measured by the number of messages, tags, or photos being exchanged. Did some friends never tag me because they didn't want to be judged as uncool? Why did this person, whom I'd always see on the socials, not reply to my post? There were many invitations for overthinking, and it made me anxious to the point where I put more time and effort into keeping up with this image of connectivity at a stressful pace. Motivation towards the daily tasks had dimmed. I was more subdued, but constantly trying to catch the attention of the other members, hoping that they would meet my eye and keep up a running joke before I found out that I wasn't meeting a target set by my teacher. I became nervous entering a circle of friends, my mind apprehending what interactions I'd missed. Something changed. My identification with other people came from my online connection with them. No one else was noticed if they weren't frequently messaging me, even if they showed a lot of decency in person. I didn't realise the problematic side, and I wondered why I wasn't reaching positive outcomes at school, before making excuses without connecting the dots to why my focus and performance wasn't the same. The cause wasn't on the map, and when I felt down from its real-life symptoms, well, guess what? I went online more. It was the welcome space to seek the gratification I believed I was getting less of than my peers. The pleasure it promised by consolidating connection made activity outside of it feel uncertain and uncomfortable. I sheltered myself from these difficulties in favour of the fantasy of mastering an online game or making my friends laugh with a meme I'd discovered. The feeling it instantly gave me made it take precedence over improving my German or going to the park on a sunny day. In my head, it wasn't a problem, it was the solution. There was plenty of time for the important tasks. *Look at it tomorrow. Just sit down and see what everyone is up to.*

1:5

"What phone do you have, Luke? I've never actually seen it before." My escape routes weren't addressing the inferiority complex I'd constructed. I wasn't one of them. I was most comfortable expressing myself in the game lobby, but I still felt further away, my inactivity late in the evening evident when all I wished to do was join my friends. It lowered my mood consistently. I'd routinely spend the school holidays staying at my grandparents with my PlayStation, knowing that I could spend unlimited time on it there, staying up very late and feeling blessed that I could join everyone online. Sometimes, my friends were offline, but I simply joined other people. A group chat was created on the socials so that we could organise sessions and share related things. Skype calls were made. My masculinity was off the leash as I participated as much as anyone else with steam blowing off me when my supercar finished first place. I was wanted, a respectable member spending hours surviving the rounds against the bots. My family gradually became concerned about the amount of time I was spending there, and their conversations grew more serious. 'Addiction' became part of the vocabulary, and I was often reluctant to sit down and do my homework.

"Sit down!" Mum demanded after I found some excuse to wander off. I was in denial, having no interest in the advice they gave for navigating through life more healthily. Eventually there were interventions, and I took it very badly. Quite literally, I was throwing the toys out of the pram, kicking and screaming, using some foul language at my mother, and then sulking for days as I despaired over the obstructions to maintaining my membership with my mates. This didn't stop me from trying though. I was totally intoxicated.

1:6

My methods of compensation for missing something made the socials very moreish to the point where I struggled to relate my immediate surroundings with the deeper feelings that mattered to my heart. I lost sight of the values around family time, or getting out of the house to do something active. These are clearly some of the foundations to live a happier life, yet I didn't take the time to reflect on it. Instead, I sat and clicked, as my picture of what people my age were doing had been contaminated by meaningless gestures and signals of visible association.

Sat in the car next to Grandpa, I heard him say, "You used to be such a happy boy. I don't know what happened to you." I didn't look him in the eye, and my gaze went ahead into the trees. No response. I had no idea what led to that. My genuine emotions were kept at bay as I was preoccupied with an electronic formula for betterment. Overall, satisfaction never came from it. I was very unhappy, and I wasn't changing my online habits at all. The only difference was that it had become a much larger behemoth that had the only say in my head on who I was and how I was doing.

Naturally, school was the base of social living, but I also had various people in my life who were outside the mix. Whether it was people I met on holiday, or friends from my football club, the online relationship began to be less intense or judgmental, because the interactions were not day-to-day, and didn't implicate social standings in the same way. I was reminded of what the socials were intended to be when I used them outside of the anxious school environment where everyone seemed to be meeting at once. It was a network that I was able to design. There was no racing element or sharp comparisons that could knock down my self-esteem.

School, at times, wasn't awful for me but the online world

completely overshadowed it, affecting every inch of my time from the start to the omnipresence of the socials. It didn't suit me, but I didn't know how to choose when it was better to let it slip by, having no safety precaution to monitor any harmful use. I never saw my situation in that light, I just wanted to play the game more.

A firm barrier had built up and I resorted to the same bunch who my online community attached me to. I began to avoid social situations that may have helped with long-run goals, not wanting to talk and get to know people from an offline setting, even if I appreciated afterwards that the opportunity was there. I was inept at bringing out the feelings until I was online, the space this ineptitude kept respawning. I was very worried about any arrangements with friends, and got depressed if they didn't go according to plan. I could have checked for hours if a meet-up would take place while it could have been called off purely because my mate wasn't feeling it after waking up on the day. One invited me for a sleepover on a Friday after school but they weren't the most loyal to me. After inviting me over, he cancelled, while I was halfway along the three-mile walk to his house. My weekend was over before it had begun, in my mental state. Every positive feeling could rest on a plan in a most illogical way, so take the plan away and I habitually thought my world was in ruins.

I was given the go-ahead before he texted me saying, "No. I said don't leave yet," followed five minutes later with, "You can't come but ask if I can stay at yours." This would have been a pain for anyone, but I found myself completely derailed. All it took was an um and an err about walking to school to set me off with my insecurity about plans. The fear made me check my phone every ten seconds, my socials too if I was at home. Since these two tools had merged, the chances of altering and cancelling plans noticeably went up, a slight change of feeling because of one little tweak in their digital-led life. I couldn't help but read more into it. *They don't like me,* I thought. *They've found a better offer. I don't have mates I can rely on. I'm alone and I don't make the cut for anyone's time.* I did nothing to prevent this sort of thinking. It was the little things that would drag down my mood, the things you tell your friends about and then get told it's nothing. It was big because of the accumulation, an upward staircase to a bigger fall – more panic as I'm further off the ground floor.

None of these feelings were revealed to anyone. I didn't think. I only wanted to keep up appearances while forgetting how to practice differently to what I was doing online. A pit was being dug deeper and deeper for burial within a wider process of people my age staying tuned for the big advances in the socials. For example, when BlackBerry Messenger (BBM) became massively popular, when its supporting smartphone was released, it affected how people interacted and how they looked at the socials. I didn't have it, and it wasn't on my mind as much as other platforms like Ask.FM or Snapchat.

But when someone put up a Facebook status saying, "Inbox me for BBM pins", there was this continuation of feeling outside the boundary to a space where people were putting their time into expressing themselves. I wasn't there, so where did I go? There were people who didn't invest themselves in these trends but this was under the radar because that wasn't evident to me from my newsfeed or my circle. If I didn't exist as much in the online world, anyone who did was superior. Since it was a picture of real-life things, photos and videos were taken. Subject matter was produced by what we thought was interesting for everyone to see. It captivated me. Standing in a special place was subordinate to the documentation of it. The moment would go because I used it on its capture rather than seeing the full picture with the naked eye. As far as I knew, I had to get that killer photo of the burger I ate in Manhattan to have a valid place on Earth, because that was what the next post about a well-presented meal would make me feel.

Besides the increasing pressure, I was watching online stars gather a massive following and expand on what they were uploading. There were live streams of gaming sessions that could sometimes last a whole twenty-four hours for fans all over the world to gather in. I said hello three times in a Twitch TV chat before the streamer said it in return. The channel turned into a full-time job. Imagine making a living out of playing games and editing recordings of winning plays! Some channels got very famous, and clearly made some people rich out of their passion projects. They were the new rock stars.

1:7

"Like and I'll rate." A friend put up this status for everyone to see.

"10. One of my best mates."

I liked and commented on his post on my wall. The next time I saw him, I warmly approached him, having felt that our friendship was totally secure after the message was sent for all to see.

"Like and I'll write," someone else put. This was a particularly popular person and I never got a post from them after liking their status. I slightly shrunk. The next time we shared a class, I didn't make eye contact, and felt anxious about being near them. *Why did I get ignored?* It was obviously likely that they ran out of time to write to everyone but I wasn't certain of this, like all the other times I didn't get a reply. *Was it rude or was it me?* Then there were videos of people doing a wacky viral activity, posting it and nominating friends for a turn. I never knew how the teachers found out, but they announced in assembly to us that anyone found to have posted a video of them downing a pint of beer with raw eggs would be excluded. It stopped this individual form, but something else always came back, a symbol of membership every time. The next form may not have promoted binge-drinking, but there was

and a lonely one at best. My position was either that, or business as usual. The next year would have me deciding between the two, according to how my emotions were reacting. Internally, things got messy.

I wasn't a teenager who regularly had lie-ins, but when I stayed up late, it was screen time. No guilt because there wasn't daylight, no need to go outside when the sun was gone. I'd chosen to reach out for an abundance of info that ate up the hours, while having no desire to put it down when my priorities were far from clear. I always liked reading books, but during an intense study week, I suspended the activity, although I still counted online activity as a part of the rest period. Everyone was fine there, right? My emotional maturity could barely regulate what this vehicle of identity really added. I lost control of what the environment could do to me, while I watched the successes of other inhabitants. It was a wheel I strongly felt, but with hands too weak to steer towards a healthier road. It all happened so fast; I had no idea where I was being taken. Was it too late to start again from the beginning to do it differently?

Before my brief spell on Instagram, I was teased in various ways that made me feel that I didn't qualify for the track that all these popular people were on, whom everyone talked about. I hadn't made the same impact as them.

A classmate asked me if I had Instagram, but before I could say anything, my mate butted in, "He doesn't have Instagram because he's a neek!" Two people I sat with at break time were exchanging updates about their aim to have more followers on Instagram than people they themselves followed. How the numbers had moved, and which names caused it, were closely studied. It helped them decide how much they were worth. While their phones were out, I made zero contributions to the conversation. The front I gave didn't match any criteria here. Whatever perception of a real player everyone had, the awkward intertwinement of the socials and my mental development didn't lead to me feeling too good when I saw the signs of this popularity game. My mates were chatting to new faces, and only a small fraction of them showed me much friendliness, while the rest went as far as condescending or ignoring the space I occupied. A tag-along or an undesirable in their eyes perhaps, a class apart from the people they approached during their social climbing pursuits. Even if someone showed a dislike towards a big name, they would still say it to suggest an association with them to leapfrog their apparent stature behind their back. It got so far deep into my head while I tried to work with the persona I'd formed. I was too tangled up to go anywhere else. However indecent, I rode the days out of encountering this kind of social behaviour without knowing if I could dissociate from it.

It was a bit of a spectator sport. The online profile was presenting who the person was to anyone who searched their name, whilst the followers were also helping to make the image. People I shared interests with were given notifications to click on that I thought would please them. And even if I disliked someone, they would still be on my friends list as a part of the numbers game. It was sometimes interesting to see their posts, an opposing degree reining in to map out the competition. Taking a break from it for a few days didn't change what it felt like when I logged on again, a light switch ready at any moment to be switched on as the electricity remains there. I failed to distinguish between image and reality, while I closely watched for the things I was missing, seeking the pleasure of interaction until I came off more uncertain every time. I lost so much more motivation because I didn't find many things to be worthwhile when I wasn't meeting the same levels of gratification. All it took was one mistake in a football match to switch me off for the rest of it. I may as well have been off the pitch. One time in my philosophy class, I was kept behind by my tutor, who asked if I really wanted to be there. That was how disengaged I was when picked to answer a question. Very few things were filling me with joy, and I was taking an awfully long time to get up and go. Once I had been such an early bird, taking a handful of minutes to wake up to the world, bright to the day's events ahead of me. Now, I tried to find a reason not to sit down and study, or take short cuts towards the bare minimum. Fewer people were conversed with, and there were no loving acts of kindness in this period for its own sake. I'd stepped into a cage of dehumanization, my technology holding me away from making something of myself. This was not who I was. How could I continue the game when there was no result that made me think that everything was going well? The cracks grew wider. Why was I acting in front of people like I was indestructible, when my own company made me think of peril?

1:9

When I was branching out with online connections at school, some of my new friends were calling me by an online gaming name. At first, I found this quite amusing, but as a part of a growing social identity, it became quite unsettling when somebody I didn't know very well would call me by it, or ask why the name was even a thing. It confined me to what that name was referring to, and made me more anxious in other areas of life. I was almost battling the thought that I couldn't be anyone else, and the worse thing was that I didn't talk about it either. It became irritating, and contributed to a growing level of angst, while the pressure to go online was a part of daily existence in a group. It was taking its toll.

Two weeks before visiting my friends, I spent more time off, but without thinking that it would be a long-term plan after the summer to address the deep-seated issues that my socials had magnified. If my senses were busy in a new place, I wouldn't dwell so much on my usual fixations. I wasn't worrying about keeping up with anyone at home. On the family holiday to New York, there was so much to see that a snap on my phone couldn't capture. For a brief period, at seventeen, I was almost enjoying something for what it was, not purely to stock up on cool things to tell everyone. If I didn't go to this landmark or that one, then it was fine, because I was enjoying myself. There were brief exceptions, like that burger, or the top of the Empire State Building, but I was spending time with my family in the city that never sleeps. I didn't have much time to sit and let the pictures of perfect people influence me in seeking the satisfaction of being someone on their terms. Instead, I found possibilities for myself, taking interest in history and culture that I naturally wanted to find out more about. It caused a deeper level of satisfaction in me to reflect on for the rest of my life. Returning to Brighton made me feel like I was meeting that same nothingness that I was distracted from addressing before I went away. It made me think about the next time I logged on, even after deliberately toning it down.

"I'll message you."

"Luke, look at the chat,"

"Message me."

"I've made a chat."

"Are you in the chat?"

"Wait, you're not in the chat, are you?"

"I'll make a new chat."

"Do you want me to add you to the chat?" Everything and more went through the group chats. Toning them down didn't change that reality. There were so many, but that was where to get clearance for what was happening next. If a group of us were talking about gathering sometime, it wouldn't be certain until it was circulated on the chat. It determined an exclusive group with its membership being frequently altered or recreated. A second social life was there, putting real life into motion and referring to it all in one. Memes were shared; pictures were sent. It was an impeccable communication tool, but I wasn't using it enough for the purpose it serves. There were parts of real life, like conversing and making the effort to meet, that were being replaced with the features of a convenient messaging platform that can be used in a variety of meaningless ways that usurp the substance of the real world. It was like filling up on sugary snacks without eating a balanced diet, if you let it. It tastes so good, but it makes it so easy for users to forget what makes the other parts of healthy living. Instant messenger is what it says on the tin, but the consumption of the service was far more complicated underneath.

I was at a friend's house party one evening, and I didn't know many people there. The people I did know there were always busy so I couldn't cling onto them. A friendly face then arrived an hour after me, and he didn't know many people either. For most of the evening, we were side by side, and I was much more comfortable being able to frequently joke with him without having to make much of an effort.

Someone then turned to us and said, "I get the sense you're both in a group chat together." I smiled with confidence. The group chat was security. From them, I knew with whom I could associate, as running jokes were made and a connection was established, even if it wasn't sincere between all the participants. From my screen, the messages would pop up for my attention and there would be a red number on the top right of the app icon on the home screen, representing the number of people/chats that had sent at least one unread message. It only took a single message to change how I approached an interaction in person. It could decide whom I was going to talk to, and how likely it was that someone would talk to me. And then if I thought I was clicking with someone, they may later behave towards me in a way that suggested that it didn't matter, since they were now with their 'real' friends in public, who

I presumed were all in a chat together. They didn't have time to greet me. I just wasn't one of them, and if I went significantly astray from my tribe, then friends would pick up on it and often cast a negative judgement.

My tablet would light up and ping. There was the option to mute it but I didn't do it in case I missed out on something. Someone changed the name of the chat. Someone sent a video to the chat. Another replied with six crying with laughter emoji's. When I clicked on a chat, there were 56 unread messages. *Oh wow! What's been going on?* I scrolled up to see who was involved and what was being discussed. There was one message after a little while saying, "What time and place?" to meet for something I was interested in. If I hadn't scrolled up, I wouldn't have found out as easily from my mates. Most of the time, I didn't receive a phone call regarding it either. I would have missed out on an entire plan if I hadn't been active on the chat.

And if I was to ask about it, sometimes one would reply, "Look at the chat. It says on there." Were they annoyed that I asked and didn't scroll up the hundreds of messages to find out the plan? Habit commanded that they didn't think to tell me individually, because that was much more of an effort and abnormal besides. I didn't have a smartphone that was powerful enough to support the separate Facebook Messenger app, so I rarely used my mobile data. Everyone else had a good enough smartphone to have the latest updated app – my technological inferiority meant I couldn't constantly check like they could. Therefore, when I went home or had Wi-Fi, there was catching up to do. It could completely dominate my routine. Checking ate up time.

When I was surgically attached to the group chat function, one thing that I was very conscious of when I opened a chat was to see who the last message was seen by. Ironically, a lot of messages in a chat were directed to an individual person more than a bunch. It was sometimes used to expose people in some way, pushing their buttons for a reaction that would decide the extent of its reappearance for every member to see. I could have been called out for seeing a message if someone was looking for me to bite back, or removed from a chat if I wasn't active for a few days. One frequent joke came up when every member of a chat had seen someone's message but no one had yet replied – the wooden spoon award of the socials. So many little things could encourage me to act out on compulsions to try and keep up. Not meeting the standard often meant getting singled out, and it wasn't branded a good look. There was even one occasion when going on a family holiday to Wales was met with a face.

"What are you going to do there?"

Deep down I knew he was just annoyed because his gamer mate was offline for a whole week. And if I made out I had homework, someone would tell me that I should do it tomorrow and he needed an extra player in the game. Comments like that were often enough to bend me to people's wishes.

Any peer pressure was exacerbated by the chats, letting it reach the safe private space and making my skin uncomfortable unless I tried to follow the pattern of my circle. In the end, my idea of the know was impossible to achieve regardless, and falling short left me believing that I was missing the biggest thing. A trigger for one moment of excitement and ecstasy made me forget how to let it go when I needed to. Enjoyment from the other things didn't come when I was thinking about what my mates were chatting about. And if they were offline, I wondered what the next interaction would be. The perpetual motion of it could momentarily make me forget who I was.

I clung to the idea that cutting it down would be temporary, and I was convinced that there would be a mountain of messages to come back to when I picked it up. I hadn't deleted the app, so I could still take a glimpse at what was popping up without clicking, feeling a massive pull to uncover exactly what the whole message contains.

That drive to be a member didn't go away just from cutting down, but my abstinence while everyone remained active only made me feel further away from the desirability or popularity that my acquaintances portrayed. I didn't even have a half-decent camera on my phone. When situations inevitably became difficult afterwards, I didn't have the socials to run back to in the same way so I couldn't refer to the current joke that quickly circulated on them. The hole that I punched left me realizing how little deeper connections I had, while this vulnerability was exposed as I entered the college cafeteria to find people to sit with. I wasn't nearly as approachable. Less talking points: less laughter, I was now more at odds than when I looked at the chats. Chatting online had originally catalysed these friendships, so taking away that base starved us of reasons to enthuse over any activity together. I was still a gamer and could receive texts from people, but this wasn't as effective in bringing me closer to what was going on. I was feeling far behind, so after a couple of months, I checked my Messenger. Disappointment. I had received far less messages. I mean why would I receive them? If I was still hanging out with people, it didn't make it the same. My whole sense of belonging had come from how I grew up besides the socials. Checking everything less was always going to correspondingly take the whole world in my mind further away. There was a dullness and a stillness that felt like an anchor had been dropped, leaving me more alone as my so-called friends drifted further on in their connected worlds. If I started up again, the stillness remained. My use did absolutely nothing to turn it around as I sunk from the real world. My misuse and abuse of the socials had gradually led to a very deep level of crisis that logging on or off couldn't change. I would go on either side of the fence for a while longer, with different pressures preventing me from leaning too far towards one side. And rather than seeking any kind of help, I watched the pressures mount up and remove the possibility of getting away from teetering on the edge. No one had a clue. I couldn't give one.

1:10

During one phase of cutting back, I tried applying for a part-time job while I was at college. My parents had suggested it but I had next to no experience so no one would hire me. I then decided to volunteer in a charity shop. When walking into town to do my weekly shift, I was thinking that it was somewhat a community service after spending so much time doing nothing particularly constructive about any real responsibilities. It was hard to know what I was addressing per se, but I was mentally unwell, and this period had me thinking more about my entry exams for university (including retakes from my disappointing first year). The college was pushing me to decide what the next step would entail. Oddly, I didn't struggle with the decision process. I think it felt so far away that I just picked one of the subjects I was already studying and made a shortlist of potential places. The only decision I seemed to care about was deferring the start date to a year later. Apart from that, my view of the future revolved around keeping up with what my mates were doing even if the nature of that was doing me harm in the present. My identity was fragile, having been formed by the socials and designed to give my peers what they wanted to see. The clothes I wore, the music I listened to, the language I used... who I was amongst my friends was very far from who I was at home. As my attention was focused on public appearances, I was under some illusion that all human eyes were camera's capturing what I looked like for everyone to see. If it was cool to be a wrong 'un then that was what I was trying to be. Big events like parties and festivals wouldn't be complete unless I got a fresh trim in the barbers the day before. Photos from the event had to feature the look. Everyone I knew was there so I had to be in the best form. I fixed my eyes on doing things for the sake of spectacle alone, totally divorced from spending time doing the things I independently enjoy. It was rarely a happy situation, but it didn't stop it from being a must. I've never been a gym lad, but there I was hitting the gym to try and get wham so that I could fish compliments from people. The less public activities like my charity work made me lay low, avoid the socials, and hide this side of me from anyone. To be contactable like them would make me give in to temptation and resume the destructive habits while I was gathering more responsibilities.

Friendship became so synthetic, and taking away the most active ingredient I've used left me feeling like none of my friends had been made naturally. The social life was constructed by the consuming efforts to maintain myself in their eyes. I was running out of energy to power up this hologram of me, and it became impossible to take my mind off it. My studies and charity work helped me learn that my social life wasn't making me feel very good. The users of the socials in person left me in the same spiral of negative self-talk. To divest time from the socials where everything was rooted would risk exile from the place I was trying to secure. My drive to power it still had the same intensity if I wanted to get out and see people.

I had next to no control. I started on the socials, and built this unsafe life with them as a youngster, so now I couldn't change what the sites were doing to me. It didn't help that I'd made myself into a terrible communicator either. Wherever I stood when I had time to observe, I saw groups of friends living their lives which made me wonder if I was really living a life while I was hanging around with these people. I may have taken part, but it was usually passive, listening to people talk about how intoxicated they wanted to be on the weekend without really having much to add. I laughed with them, I made references and opinions about the football or a newly released song, but I wasn't an independent player. I didn't have friends at mine, or make suggestions about the next activity we should do together. I was following the crowd, a sheep shepherded in the herd. My will was absent, my mind totally preoccupied with an image I knew I'd found no success in maintaining. In a group call one evening, I was pressed into looking at my newsfeed and a group chat, before telling them that I wasn't aware of any of the content they were referring to.

"How have you not seen it!?" one exclaimed.

"Are you living under a rock?" another quipped. A whole world as one, and my feeling of membership within it seemed constantly endangered. I couldn't afford to let people know I was outside of it. When trying to plan a group holiday for the summer after finishing college, the ideas were always changing. No one really agreed on how to do it. My semi-withdrawal from the chats was putting me in the dark. I wasn't helping with cooperation as I failed to see the difference between euphoric sensations, and genuinely important conversations. One day, I was chatting with a classmate who knew my friends and he broke the news to me that it was something entirely different to what I believed was the final plan. I was so embarrassed to be told by someone who wasn't even going with us, my dissociation playing out in an otherwise ordinary interaction. My friends assumed that I knew what was going on because it was spoken about on the chat.

Then, when one noticed that I hadn't been active there for a few weeks, he texted me, "You need to look at the chat." That was it. Out for dinner with my parents, I panicked. My phone couldn't look up all the messages. *What had I missed? Were they about to book it all?* I couldn't do that there and then. Rather than call him or ask for an explanation as to what was going on, I waited until I got home that evening, thinking and worrying until I was able to check. If I wanted to keep up with this big plan for the summer after turning eighteen, then I'd have to look. It was all happening too fast to catch up in-person. One call would probably leave me with more questions than answers, before the chat sped away from everyone's thinking from the day before. The trip was booked, but

I didn't really get involved in the decision-making process, preferring to sit back, to cope with the stress of my situation. I still wanted to go. The flights were booked at extremely awkward times – the return was at about six in the morning the day after we packed up and left the festival. This was months away, so no one immediately cared about having to wait in a terminal all night before getting on the plane. We were lazy when we preferred to do it all via the chat, so we didn't think. The exchange between the six of us was so fast that I didn't really have time to find all the important details within the haystack of all the usual unrelated stuff. Big chats made for messy plans. We spent far more time on the chat, fantasizing about a crazy lads' holiday. The socials were centre stage. All our attention was focused on it, the talking points were more of an effort to follow through when you could make fun out of a situation with a meme without thinking too hard. As much as I silently tried to reduce my investment in them, the magnetic pull was powered by real individual people, and it became clear to me how big the void could be once I discovered all the interactions I'd missed. I was beginning to experience the withdrawal symptoms of backing off after years of abuse. It was like I poisoned my brain so that I couldn't find any pleasure without clicking the next notification. Even the social features of other apps, like Spotify, were starting to bring it all to the same whole unit in my mind, dulling my senses to the importance of anything I had to do outside its frame. Now my further dissociation was making me feel like I was going backwards, even if I was spending more time with my studies. I logged onto something to at least try to satisfy my greedy appetite for the indulgences that swept me away. I played games without checking my friends list but it felt a bit pointless, since I wasn't performing in the social life that dragged me there in the first place. If I briefly checked a chat for a significant plan, I entered a rabbit hole and had to fight very hard not to click on something unimportant. My reach was infinite for the social features, but so limited for the true relationships that I had left. Real life felt rubbish, so I didn't work to alleviate myself from the puddle of mud I splattered all over myself which represented my recurrent dysthymia. My foreseeable options for refuge were shrinking.

1:11

Naturally, the path of an eighteen-year old's social life often led to the night out. It became the hottest topic on the socials, grouping together people who enjoyed the same musical styles so I ended up going to clubs that played intense dance music without thinking about who was playing but simply trying to follow where the excitement drifted in my urban environment. There were arrangements I didn't see coming. My original circle had brought in other faces whom I didn't get to know well, before being thrown in with them, not feeling like I was approachable unless they wanted to follow a profile which displayed what I was worth. It made me anxious, so I failed to really click with them, despite often seeing them around. I was therefore the least likely to upload the pictures or videos of young people having fun in the evening. My self-esteem became so far low that I wasn't usually willing to greet them, knowing that making the effort without Instagram would be a waste of time. I continued convincing myself that I wanted to be there though, exposing myself out there so at least I could say I was doing something with young people. But whatever part of who I was before my bad habits with the socials, this was a part that wasn't out at all. It was a part of me that seemed incapable of coming to life in the world as I'd experienced it. The image I had created was running out of energy, failing to keep up the superficial gestures of a busy milieu. My will to keep up with social appearances was faltering as I heavily reduced my effort to maintain the adequate profile that had always seemed above me. There were events coming up. *Should I bail? Would anyone be bothered if I didn't go? What impact was I really going to make on leading the fun for everyone?* Well, I continued trying. I was flying to another country with these people, so I had to continue. There were a lot of people going there from Brighton. They were going to see me, so I still had to work out at the gym. I had to continue with the friends I had, even if our bond was looking weaker by the week. I'd known some of these people for years. We played games and joked for hours together. I couldn't retreat. It was all supposed to be fun, but a lot of it involved tagging people with pictures and liking posts. There was no resisting going to the things that they enjoyed, or I simply wouldn't be living at all.

My grandparents had bought me an iPhone for my eighteenth birthday, the world's most popular smartphone, with its iconic user-friendly format, all on one little device. The phone, the computer, the ultimate tool of connectivity – I had something that had the power to impress my mates with its technological prowess. It was many people's symbol of modern life just like the car used to be. In my unstable condition from my relationship with its services, I carried a fully capable model like all my other acquaintances. Awesome. If only I could have used it well.

I began to view some of my friends' relationships with the socials as bizarre, but laughed with them when they joked about my peculiar identity on them. The last year had made some differences begin to show from the outside. Why was my mate taking a video on their phone of a music artist playing their most popular tune? It was probably distracting them more than it was distracting me. But then without thinking, I was taking a video of a climax when I was once at the front of the crowd for a DJ set. I knew that was what people did, so when I was there in a spot where someone may have done it, I mimicked it without a thought. Not to do it would make my experience less than theirs. Someone standing behind me jokingly put their finger on the stop button of my screen and I let them do it because I realised that what I was doing felt ridiculous. I'd behaved in that way because all the people behind me could see me appear to be in a special place. I didn't even like the DJ. There was no fulfilment, only foolishness.

1:12

During that long night's wait at the terminal in Alicante airport, my friend vented about not being able to get any data on his smartphone at the tail end of the week-long trip. I questioned whether there was any need, since we had so much to excitingly reflect on.

"I need to know what's happening in the world," he answered. If it had been put less emphatically, then I wouldn't have thought that looking at his newsfeed couldn't possibly be that important.

It was a few months after I began to check my socials far less, and on our journey home, when we stopped at an internet café, my other friend exclaimed, "There are so many music videos to catch up with." They checked YouTube to see who had released what. Interests like music had been transferred to a colossal supply of content. You could never watch it all. Or could you? I was observing someone catching up excessively without realizing that my habits had been similar. My perception of someone using it like me undermined the harmful nature of my individual experience. My social intentions were completely misled by the unguided mind of a teenager trying to feel like they had a place with people of the same age. Every proud moment could be celebrated on the socials with a ceremonial display sent to all, but now I was weary that I had got hooked to the idea of it, and torn apart by it, at the same time. The emotional reality began to leave me muted to everyone too.

Imagine losing your voice, but being able to talk at the same time. You're saying words, but no one can quite hear you. If they occasionally heard you, what you were saying wasn't taken seriously. There would be a short answer that kills the conversation, or you'd be ignored. Your mum, your dad, your social butterfly friend all walk off. They get back to what they were thinking about before, chatting with someone else in the vicinity or putting their head down to read something like their phone.

My ability to communicate had become so poor that I would often say things I didn't mean or repeat words someone said to me earlier only to get an inch of attention. I still followed my crowd, stressing that my former intimate relationship with the socials could never lead me on the same level as anyone. I never moved on my own accord because it seemed invalid. This wasn't a life. No one was going to look at me like an equal so I wasn't an equal. Invites to hang out were rarely one to one and only because I was there anyway. I was supposed to meet early with a friend who lived near to me before a local festival but they didn't call me. It turned out his phone was broken and he told no one else to phone in his place. When I phoned another friend, I heard crowds cheering in the background while being informed that everyone was there. I rushed to the rough location I was directed in the searing summer heat. My phoneless friend was enjoying himself and I stood on the other side of the group, feeling unwanted. I recognised many faces around me, and strove desperately to look like I was having fun. The company gathered to get to the main stage but then I was asked to wait by someone who needed the toilet just as everyone else was rushing off. I waited there, feeling irrelevant, after my day had already been shaken up in disarray, then he re-joined me.

"Come on, let's catch up with them!" he said, before speeding off a few steps ahead of me. When I saw him catch the tail end of the group, I stopped following him. I was at a halt while I watched them all walk away from me. The event had begun to build up, but I turned back, and walked away in the opposite direction with my head down. It was at that point, where I lost the will to carry on with everybody. There wasn't a single part of me that wanted to be there on that day. My imagination of social living had paused, and I stopped thinking about what emotional baggage would come afterwards. I really wanted to be out there and be a person according to a set of measures of success in the virtual world. It was the custom I knew best but I wasn't doing it for this. I wasn't enjoying this place; I wasn't properly connecting with anyone here. I finally gave up. I told Mum that I felt like leaving early but said nothing more about the day. For some reason I had a panic attack when a couple of my friends were calling me interchangeably. In my mind, there was nobody for them to reach, so when they tried to reach me, I let it ring. The phone went on complete mute. No vibrations included. It was out of sight. Trouble and embarrassment were the only things to come from it. I deleted the apps for my socials the day afterwards. My phone was put in a drawer without it being checked. The life I'd built for myself represented nothing to me that meant anything positive. It was all too much for me. Technology had taken over me at my invitation as a host, connecting me only with mental harm that spiralled more and more. My time spent with it did immeasurable damage. I needed to stay away from it so that I could feel better. Going offline meant I had to withdraw from being out in public. I thought I could do better with using it, but it kept getting worse and worse. I was so twisted up; I didn't know how to live with or without it while life outdoors with young people was moving fluidly from its capabilities. I had no coping mechanism available for myself, no idea how to talk to anyone about the thing that made all my problems worse. The need for membership was disastrous. It wasn't abandoned forever in my head, but on that day, everything had stopped both off and online. Going into hiding became the only course my shrouded vision could see. I just hoped that everything was going to be okay.

Part II

2:1

I was still tuned the same, but the snowball stopped rolling. Perplexed and horrified, I didn't know what to call what was happening in there, but something was. *Mental preoccupation? Or what? And how?* By then, there was no denial inside me as to where this nameless thing was coming from. It had been put miles away, like every single individual on the lists. I couldn't get my head around the process, but everything else inside me said, *Stop!* The role I saw in it for other people's lives left me worrying so much, but my efforts to address it only left me more depressed. Naivety kept telling me that illness was being sick, or getting a flu – something in your body that declares war on your immune system and sabotages everything to the point that your body releases stuff associated with being below 100%. What I was experiencing didn't follow suit. The phone and the online world weren't a bug or an infection. It was the socials. Ordinary life. People move around as they connect, but that was why all of this felt so much worse. I'd never felt this bad during a bout of sickness or injury. The socials had been worse for me than all of the above. They had to be put away along with anything that carried them. Anything loosely connected had to go. That also meant the people there were part of the danger. *Everything must go. But now, why wasn't that making me feel better? I'm not 100%, call it 35.* I had no idea how to make sense of it, so I panicked and went to a whole new extreme at the opposite end of physical attachment.

I had no knowledge of the extent that my social life with the socials had left me imbalanced, with no protection against any misuse. I thought everyone online had a better life than me, and my end to the search for improvement was the final straw for putting me down in the dirt. My family did raise concern. They could all see that I wasn't the happiest child and that real life was dampened by my attitude to virtual life, but I never took their worries seriously. They weren't a part of this, not having been confronted with interactive media of this propensity back in the day. My idea of connectivity didn't include them in it as they helplessly approached the issue. There were no expert eyes on what this kind of networking could do to how we saw ourselves in relation to others. Very little was preventing me from latching all my senses onto the content of the screens that had transformed everyone's lives. Whatever my life was from the age of thirteen to eighteen was abruptly traversed away from facing the outdoors. But the shock of that change was like an earthquake out of this world. The only light that I would have for a very long time was the promise to myself that I could come back a better person. In the meantime, everyday life mainly consisted of looking forward to going to sleep at night. I didn't want to be seen unless my image was salvaged; connected to all the others to belong to a space for everyone gathering messages to plan the next great thing. I was frightened of where I was going without maintaining what I had. I knew the socials weren't going to stop because I did. All its members were racing away, while I was left a disgrace behind them.

I didn't go on my games console. My tablet, mp3 player, smartphone, and all my chargers were put in a drawer in my bedroom. Everything was considered a part, and now I was nothing but an empty case. The corner of my mind was saying: *There's no good to come out and make an impact on people's lives. Saying please and thank you at a minimum is futile when I'm this useless. I'm a stupid boy who lost everything that theoretically should have helped me. Departing from the online world has taken me away from any possibility of being someone now.* Darkness fell. *I'm alone and completely lost with no one to reach out to. People can't read minds so this secret has turned me into a lost cause after ending the pursuit of unreachable goals for glory.* Now that the situation led here, I wasn't sure what was keeping me going. Nothing could be done without reintroducing myself to virtual life, however harmful that proved to be. I failed to live healthily beside it, and now without it in my hands, I still felt the same, if not worse. Sat at my desk, my chest felt very tight. The window to the right looked out at the city lights and I saw my reflection on the panes. Everywhere I looked made the inside of my head burn as I saw nothing around me that wasn't squashing any idea of hope. I wasn't sure I could live with this. My will was fading as I began to conclude that there was nowhere to move to make everything better. Only worse. No talking though. I passively existed and waited to be well enough to go back to something. What thing? *Nothing,* the same corner of my mind said, *I'm worth nothing.*

Who's saying that? There's no one else in the room.

You are, and you know yourself best. I stood up, switched off the light and lay down on my bed. The dialogue remained the same. A crescendo of doom had built up to this miserable finale with its outro leading me to a wide hole of nothingness from my deliberate dissociation from the world. As soon as my head hit the pillow, I felt the full sensation of it flowing through my veins and seeping out to envelope me in a blanket of blue. Where next? I didn't think I was going to last much longer.

2:2

What I did was walk. I took long walks each afternoon, where I knew no one from my life would see me. The walks took me along the Sussex coastline, and however wet and grey it was at times, time was killed. A lot of miles were travelled along the chalky cliffs. I sat on benches for a while, staring into the sea, wondering what percentage of the mental damage was left to heal. After that, I headed back home, ate the dinner that Mum cooked, and went straight up to my room without saying a word – the saddest metaphor of Timbuktu ever. Staring at the walls around me as I put my head on the pillow again, the same unwelcome thoughts rolled in. They held a grip on me, filling me with ideas of how I may have succeeded had the socials not been so detrimental to my health. After about an hour, I was in the existential present, where I felt the weight of how far I'd fallen from life. I paid too much attention to the wrong things on there, and therefore allowed a whole world to consume me.

"What have I done?" I whispered.

I lost interest in watching TV. Streaming things or seeing any media coverage had no purchase despite it being an activity I used to frequently do with my family. Anything current was rarely picked up on my radar because it all had a similar psychological presence about it. I wanted it out of the window. My disjointed reality became so harsh that I did everything to avoid digital interpretation. Even my parents' radio got a little uncomfortable at times, making me anxious to enter the kitchen. What was left? Sometimes I sat at my desk playing solitaire.

I did at least have a job, even if it was mostly part-time. Fortunately, it began when I had my phone on, so it became valuable considering the code of today's professional conduct requiring you to be contactable for interview. I wasn't spending, so

online when my relationship with it made me cease to live. Agoraphobia took the place of my former online life. I didn't want to have contact anymore.

Administration is performed digitally. Exchanging information and messages entailed software by necessity. That was the rule. My unfollowing cast me out of any place to go. I didn't have the expertise to explain why using one of my accounts or devices caused a meltdown. *How weak is that?* Getting out of bed was hard work with the self-loathing that followed this analysis.

2:3

There was no time to put my head down or cross the road. I bumped into two people I used to hang around with and one of them was very annoyed.

"Where have you been?" I predicted there was an event coming up so I asked if they were going.

The offended one sneered, "Yeah the tickets have sold out mate, we got them ages ago." The other one asked if I wanted to hang out but I immediately said that I couldn't. Then they told me to get on Facebook again. It was the natural place to resume the association as I'd known it. That was how it worked. It was the world we all knew. I attempted to brush off the demand, using slang to say how stupid it was.

"What?" they laughed. I made a gesture that it was time for me to go and we parted ways. I noticed my hands were shaking. A flight mechanism had come into play here. At the festival, I made an active decision at that moment to cut myself off. Now this fear was telling me that I wanted to be cut off indefinitely. All of it got torn apart while I didn't have the strength to make another draft. Limbo.

At my grandparents' house, my family were talking about a

video cassette tape that had a recording of my first ever Christmas. Eighteen years later, we were all sitting around the TV during the festivity, watching me play with the encouragement of my parents. It was a blast from the past that made me sit still as I stared at the start of the horror that was my life while all my family around me were entertained by the footage. *Look at what I've become?* My reaction was so opposed to the rest of the room. I was so far away from the joy around me. *I've failed everybody.* I started off around so much love, only to reach a blackout scenario where nothing in front of me was right. More than anything, I wanted to rewind back to the day that footage was made and go from there. Later that evening on the 25th of December, I begged to go back to it. *Please.*

Two days later, I overheard a conversation between my parents' midway through.

"I don't know why Luke hasn't been seeing his friends lately. I think something might be wrong," Mum said.

"I've known for quite some time that something's wrong," Dad replied.

"Maybe he's being cyberbullied." I quickly backed away. The conversation seemed like it was in a reality I didn't understand. It was so far away from me, like a distant digging above an underground cavern. Mum later came into my room and asked why I wasn't seeing anyone.

"Nothing. Nothing's wrong, Mum. I'm not being cyberbullied. If I was being cyberbullied then I'd tell you." It was too easy to be vague if she pressed further, regardless of my lack of conviction. In truth, I couldn't put me and the socials into words. My parents had already become accustomed to me not being open about my feelings as a teenage boy. Nothing was making the secret come out, so I told myself to endure until the day I hoped to live again.

I didn't like being seen walking aimlessly through the city on my own. If someone glanced at me in the street, it felt like I shouldn't be there. Existing without the internet now relegated me to a shadow. I suddenly became very conscious of the tingling sensations in my arms and legs. *What was I doing here, if not living? What was it that kept my internal organs going when any movement from a human in front of me transmitted to my brain that I'm a waste of space.* My heart was still pumping blood around my body. The oxygen in the atmosphere continued to be inhaled inside. Was it possible to be so lost that these bodily processes simply stop? I put two fingers on the inside of my wrist, and imagined the source to go on strike.

"Sorry, you're not giving us good reason to work anymore. There'll be disruption unless you make some serious changes." Well, the change wasn't going to come from anyone else. No one was going to find me; I could only stop myself from being lost. This kind of dialogue was a weekly occurrence. It filled the space left from the guiding forces of the socials towards constructing a self. Occasionally I would look up identity in the dictionary, there was that much not so free time to think about everything without any events to consolidate it. Mum was telling me that I must do something otherwise I'd get bored. The duration of my illness was beyond belief. *When will it end?* I wasn't sure if I could bear this any longer. There was nothing I was passionate about that I could pour my soul into. I paced my room for hours waiting for the afternoon to end. No bad dream I'd ever had could resemble anything like this.

That instant access picture of the outside world is a staple of modern life like bread and butter. Life is made more interesting. You can search up anything that corresponds with key words from your passions and then be handed links to countless sites that often try to cater for your shopping tastes too. My version of this picture hadn't been updated for half a year by February 2017. It was a memory, not a refreshed page, and therefore my world had shrunk. Any temptation to re-enter the world in online terms filled me with fear. I'd closed the floodgates, and there was a lot of information on the other side. It didn't matter what it was: the latest games, recent terrorist attacks, *Game of Thrones* spoilers, deadly natural disasters, anything and everything would feel like it came from one branch if I went on one platform, and it would overwhelm my brain to the point where I'd have to sit outside for an hour with a cup of tea. It was that sensitive. Against my wishes, I couldn't compartmentalise any of it into different levels of importance. Psychologically, the infinite GBs of data was a single unit connected to the trauma and dysfunction I'd experienced from my use of it as a developing child. Highly irrational, but it couldn't be controlled. Whereas, if content was shared through word of mouth, then it's separate from the monstrosity I'd created. But then it had also given me huge trust issues. These triggers had guaranteed that using the web in the conventional way wouldn't make a fit and prosperous relationship with me. Loads of people live online to the point that they are dependent on it, but I couldn't delete my history with it. No aspiration could prepare me to pick it up again in the same way. I looked at myself in the mirror like I was testing my mirror self-recognition. I remained unimpressed. *Look at what you've done to yourself. You're an emotional wreck. Stay off and keep trying to fix up.* I was sad when I hovered near that clifftop, or busy road crossing, but I also felt an energy that made me determined to see this through. *If I could get myself here in this mess, then I can turn it around. I chose to go offline, didn't I?* Something must have changed. The walks continued.

2:4

As the empty months brought me to spring, there was added expectation to finally get travel ideas into play as that was the story I wanted to tell my family about my gap year. Eventually, my delays prompted Mum to grab me a brochure from an agency. I was grateful for the opportunity to browse offline, but I hesitated to give it a good look. It was targeted towards young adults, and seeing pictures of them having a good time with people in various places made me feel inadequate because I was an eighteen-year-old who hadn't had fun with younger people. The idea of booking to go on something on my own was way out of my depth. I was out of touch. Looking at the section about Italy, there was a rough itinerary on each option to make its features look appealing to adventurers. At the end of the page, it read that you were saying farewell to your new friends after exchanging online profiles. That last bit terrified me. It looked like an expected outcome for the agency's customers. Going on a trip had my interest no doubt, but I didn't believe I was capable of what my family were pushing. I couldn't even use a mobile. How was such a mentally disturbed individual going to possibly be able to do this? Before I could say no, Mum rang the agency and booked me an appointment. Once I entered the office, I could barely voice an opinion. I spent the meeting with the advisor in a big single office space on the high street, with other young travellers also in appointments around me. I listened and nodded, then said yes to go on a two-week tour of a stretch of Italian landmark cities. This alone was the most eventful thing I'd done in my gap year so far. It firmly put into perspective how stressful and scary it was to try and rehabilitate myself back into a world I left when becoming practically off the grid. It showed me how far I'd withdrawn, and now I was diving headfirst into a trip abroad all on my own. More difficulty lay ahead before I had set off. I had to get my tablet back out; the trip depended on it. Booking flights… check. I breathed again. Currency … Mum was suggesting I use a multi-currency card that I'd used the summer before, but I couldn't get into my online account to transfer any money. With my parents advising that this was the most effective way of getting a good exchange rate, I was in a panic as I reset the password before having to contact a helpline. No avail. I dropped the tablet with a loud thud, then went for a walk. It cost me more money in the long run, but luckily my usual card allowed me to withdraw local currency abroad. It had to do. I don't think I could have sorted it out online. It wasn't worth it. The days were running out before the trip, but I still wasn't well while I had to book transport from Leonardo Da Vinci Airport to the meet-up point in Rome. The distance between the two was significant, so it became another mission. I forced myself to go on a phone call with the agency, seeing as it was possible to book a transfer through them. The same advisor I'd met in store picked up and it was a disaster. I was shaking like a leaf and failed to sufficiently explain what I wanted. After the most broken conversation ever, I'd managed to book the transport, although I thought that something wasn't right.

"Are you sure the return journey is included?" I suddenly found my voice. The advisor claimed they'd checked and it was, but I wasn't wholly convinced about the apparent bargain once I'd put down my mobile. I decided to let it slide, and a wave of relief came from the belief that I didn't have to use anything else before the journey. My phone and tablet went back in draw 101. It was slammed shut and I breathed again.

With three days to go before I flew out, I looked at the state of my hair and pictured embarrassment to come. I'd kept up good hygiene and cleanliness during my darker period, but I didn't see the point in going to the barber. There was no appearance to keep, no fresh trim required to pay for when I wasn't out in the world. Braving the talk with a stranger and asking them for something that would affect the way you look was unlike anything. I went somewhere local. They were only taking appointments, so I said yes to an available slot on the spot, since I didn't want to do anything with the phone.

One day to go, and my gut was telling me that perhaps I should check if anyone was contacting me regarding the trip. My tickets were thankfully posted to me or printed out, but an email was sent to me the day after I'd booked my shuttle from the airport. I saw what it read and swore. The advisor who'd served me said that it turned out there wasn't a return ticket included so she'd cancelled the booking. After the otherwise small mistake, she'd tried to contact me to rebook before it was too late, but of course, I didn't have the capacity to look out for the twist. I had a glimpse at the other emails around it that included Facebook group chat messages, fuelling my string of curses at the distressing realization that I had no way of getting from the airport to the tour. I informed my parents, without the part where the agency had emailed me before it was too late. Naturally, they were outraged, and took it out on the advisor. At 10 pm on a Saturday, Mum managed to get through to an emergency helpline for the tour company, to learn that I could get a transfer from the airport at a reasonable price without booking. By the end of this rollercoaster, I could finally calm down less than twelve hours before my flight, but I was already exhausted from jumping the hurdles towards it. Then the sleepless night of shaking anxiety came in. I was nineteen, and I was taking a big leap from existential collapse to a solo trip abroad. This wasn't merely being out of my comfort zone.

"Make sure you text us when you land," Mum told me before dropping me at the airport. Well, I had to take my phone then, didn't I?

2:5

Right, so I'm in an unfamiliar place and a lot of people around me have got their phones out to organise what they're doing with themselves. My expectations didn't change the way that reality hit me. People were looking up destinations or arranging transport all over. I strolled attentively after grabbing my baggage, moving past a series of drivers who each had paper signs held up on display. I wish.

Someone then popped into my periphery. "Taxi?" I obviously looked a little lost, so my attention was darting around. It was tempting but I knew it was going to cost a fortune. I had the address I was heading to on paper. It was lucky my parents hadn't fully embraced keeping all details digitised. I was always going to butcher pronouncing it properly anyway. I walked past different shuttle bus kiosks with queues in front and I thought to myself: *I should go further in case there was more.* In the end, I had to turn back. *Wow, I'm already behaving aimlessly.*

I half-heartedly approached a uniformed staff member.

"Yes, where would you like to go?" He read the address in my hands and gave me a price. It was almost double that which the travel agent had quoted. I started and the staff read my body language.

"One moment please," he turned to his company kiosk. A slightly better deal returned but it wasn't great. They claimed it was that way because my destination wasn't in the town centre. I couldn't be bothered to consider if I was being a bit ripped off. At this point, I just wanted to get to the destination and cool off the adrenaline.

I'd travelled with family and friends before, but this was uncharted territory. The guide for the whole tour was standing in the lobby of the hotel. He was going to be leading over fifty different people from English-speaking countries. After I shakily introduced myself, he gave an air of making sure accountability for what I did was in my hands, despite there being a super busy itinerary. Before talking to him, I saw two young people move on towards the lobby's elevator. Was I going to be the only one arriving on my own? I felt a shadow covering me that hadn't gone away since Mum said goodbye to me at the airport. My hotel room was vacant when I entered. There was supposed to be a roommate with me for the duration of the tour but there were no other personal belongings inside. I texted Mum to say that I had arrived safely and put my phone deep into my suitcase, but then a new wave of insecurity hit me. *I'm really not sure about this.* It would have been much more comfortable to be told what to do. That way I wouldn't have been required to use my own initiative in a skin that felt zero individuality in its cargo. I looked out the window pensively then decided to leave the room and find the part of the building where the guide mentioned to meet. This was the most nervous I'd been in my whole life, but I had to find people. I arrived early and there was only a bunch of four together. I began on a table alone, before someone asked me in a Yorkshire accent if I wanted to join theirs across from mine. I tried to tell them my name, but I stammered before sitting down so I froze on the chair in an awkward position.

Once the room filled up, the guide gave a talk ending with him asking everyone to stand up one by one and: "Say your name, say where you're from, say what you're passionate about." The meaning of stage fright got taught to me, but I was here now, whether I liked it or not. *Ride it and see what happens.* For a few seconds I wanted to contract but my roommate came to the rescue at the perfect time.

An hour before, I was freaking out, but that all seemed stupid once we got talking. It was a big jump, but it proved to be pivotal in relearning what a decent conversation was with another young person. I suppose that's the entry point wherever you are : talking. Access confirmed, and I could have an adventure. My introversions weren't gone by magic, but the occasion forced me to barge through them as best I could. This is what a gap year was really for, not that long wait before I stood up to the moment. People were here to meet others from around the globe. There were plenty of solo travellers like me, but this didn't matter. Everyone was open to new things, an inspiration I more than needed to see. As it turned out, I was the youngest on the tour. I had the choice of what excursions captured my interests or where I would like to wonder when we had free time, almost always in the company of others. This was a good balance considering I didn't have a great sense of direction and my experience at the airport made me want to latch onto people. The guide's phone number was given, but I intended to avoid resorting to that. There were other pressures as I anticipated there would be. A Facebook group was set up for members of the tour to join and perform the usual stuff of coordinating or sharing pictures. The guide was trying to encourage everybody to add each other on the socials, since that was where people looked to represent a new friendship. I ignored the subject and relished my safe reason for wanting to stay off any of that throughout an action-packed trip. It was accepted and once or twice complimented, but people still asked. That was custom, but the conversation was easy to brush aside when there was this much substance for my senses to absorb from enjoying Italy. The day after arrival, we took a coach to Pompeii to see the Roman ruins. For some reason, I decided to take my phone with me. I guess I wanted to at least pretend to be an ordinary person for the time being.

Despite all the anxiety, my awe at the ancient remains left me thinking, *okay, I should probably take a few snaps on my phone, shouldn't I?* One glimpse at the home screen and I saw texts from both my parents asking me if I had arrived safely and that they were worried. *What!?* I had to open the messages even though I was having a panic attack. My body squirmed in the beating sun as I was still trying to follow the proceedings. Maybe this is a feeling like what the residents of Pompeii were experiencing as they were about to be buried by volcanic ash all those centuries ago. I saw the text I tried to send hadn't gone through to Mum and I almost swore out loud next to other members of the tour. A quick text to Dad and then I turned the phone off and breathed. That was enough distraction from this world heritage site. I just wanted to enjoy the rest of it without any trouble.

I was astonished to find that the people I was touring Italy with were not concerned with doing things to appear more interesting. It was a different dynamic here. The only exception was my roommate's push towards trying out all the excursions without holding back. He was a seasoned traveller so taking yourself out to the experience was some valuable advice that timelessly stood unfazed by the ubiquitous striving to document experiences on a smartphone. I furthermore put myself down for everything I could, while a bunch of friendly young people made it even better. This was what I was saving up for in the abyss. At least some of the time, I could forget the constant discomfort I had known from being a screw loose at home.

2:6

Upon arriving at Sorrento in the evening, I hadn't clocked that everyone was dressing up for dinner and my realisation came when we made eye contact. This was the first time I properly saw her, and I felt a bit self-conscious in my cap and T-shirt which had become quite sweaty from the walk around Pompeii. As I entered the restaurant with everyone, I heard a gasp in front of me. There was an expansive balcony overlooking the Bay of Naples, with Mount Vesuvius's smoky tip providing a backdrop on the horizon to the urban sprawl across the water. While everyone went up to the railings to take pictures, I sat on one of the empty booked tables, a large round one with twelve seats. Moments passed before I turned to the left and saw the girl slowly approach my table to sit on the next chair left of me. I instantly took my gaze away out to the bay without greeting her. Her roommates soon saved her from my guarded reserve, sitting on the other side of me chatting loudly with one another. It was far less awkward when my roommate sat at the table, making an entrance on the other side from my love at first sight.

"Would you like some wine?" the person to my right asked as she grabbed a bottle from the table. I tried to answer but barely anything came out. The girl quickly looked at me, before sharply darting her head away to pretend not to hear my fragile attempt to answer the yes or no question. I said very little throughout the meal. My roommate went into a story about our night out in Rome, asking me if I wanted to tell a funny part of it, although I passed the buck straight back to him, too afraid that I wouldn't be able to manage more than a nervous stammer. As he brought me into the conversation, the girl locked her eyes into mine in a way that was unforgettable. I hadn't realised the depth of what I was experiencing, my focus taken away towards making less of a fool out of myself. A phone came out for a group selfie, and I shuffled over to get in shot, feeling the sensitivity as I saw her body language show that she noticed me move an inch closer to her. The months in total darkness couldn't prepare me for this.

As the tour walked the next morning, I knew she was beside me without turning my head. I recognised her from her shadow on the ground in front of the sunshine. I attempted to start a conversation, making a comment on the landscape in a low tone before the tour boarded a ferry to head to the island of Capri. So much beauty around me. She was always interested in whatever I had to say, however minimal. My newfound sense of humour made her laugh, and she tried to mirror it even when I was the only one in the circle laughing back. Once everyone stopped on a beach to explore at leisure, I turned around as I headed towards the sea and saw her sat on the pebbles watching me with a smile that shone a light in my life. I'd never imagined this was possible, wishing so badly that I was ready to meet this wonderful person.

There was an ineptitude in opening up. Since I'd become

accustomed to a world that poured personal details onto a smartphone, I failed to see the person in me that could effectively relate to other people. The socials were for affirmation, and now I was learning the hard way how to deal with it without them, highly sensitive of any external activity that was associated with their deployment. I was hideously camera shy, feeling totally uncertain of what was being seen on the screen from the phone camera. When we all checked into a hotel, I was very conscious that an awful lot of people were often asking for the Wi-Fi code before doing anything else, even collecting their room keys. It meant I sometimes had more time to kill in an interval, but I only braved a solo wonder once, wary that when I left people's company, I was very much disconnected from the world. When conversing over landmarks, fellow travellers said that they would put their pictures on the Facebook group. The girl's roommate asked me if I was in the group then urged me to join it.

"Yeah, you should!" the girl echoed afterwards. Her smile was getting me every day. I did manage to get to know her a fair amount. She liked cats. She liked thrashy rock music. She liked Harry Potter. I liked those things too. After our stop at Venice, I found myself averting from the pursuit, but I was fully aware about how fast the whole trip was going. One moment we would talk and laugh as the tour stopped by the Grand Canal next to the Rialto Bridge, then a newmade friend asked what my plan was for the evening.

"Let's go somewhere to eat," I said, then I darted off after I saw the scowl on her face, as I left her company in this glamorous setting. My flight mechanism was too fast for me to comprehend my desire in the moment. I went for the secure option instead. In Milan, I connected better, but only to then falter and leave her roommate panicking when the girl vanished for a length of time during the night. When we found her, she claimed that she was by the bar the whole time despite us looking everywhere. She wasn't looking too pleased, and her roommate left us to it. There was a constant tension in me between my new obsession and the disorder within. On a ferry in the Italian Riviera, I watched her a few benches away staring out into the water on her own, while I thought about my own mental barrier impeding me from trying to consolidate such a prospect for emotional connection. When I commented that I hadn't taken many photos, she replied that she'd send me some. I felt the pressure of time more and more while I was running out of it to step up, but I wasn't there. On the last night, I said my farewells to a bunch that included her. The last thing I saw before dashing off was her smile again. It was a smile that made me feel real when I was only a fraction of myself. Whatever I failed to do, I would remember the feelings it put inside of me for the rest of my life.

The next morning, I sat having breakfast with some of the others from the tour and asked the person sat next to me if they could add me to the Facebook group with an intense difficulty that was pulling my face apart.

She snorted, "You have to add me first." I quickly logged into the hotel's Wi-Fi on my phone, everything racing in my mind but not pulling me away from battling the nameless once more. I briefly saw my news feed and the number of notifications on my profile. It was impossible not to. Managing to add the neighbour on the table didn't quite make me certain of being across the line, however. I requested to join the group but the person who'd set it up had to approve it. I got irritable suddenly, and it implicated my goodbyes to the table. When I got to the airport, I was with two of the others before they caught their flight back to Canada. One of them tried to add me on Facebook after I told him he'd be able to find me on the group. I tried asking him if he had but didn't get a clear answer face to face. I was left uncertain whether I was in the group or not, my insecurity of connectivity experiencing some heavier tremoring. We said goodbye with a big embrace that suggested future contact, but then I was the lone shadow again, going on the plane to fly out of Italy back to Britain.

My head was spinning from the intense struggle to compute. As I began to process everything about that trip on the plane home, I finally appreciated my fatigue. Regardless of the discomfort, I made myself go on the socials on the last morning because I wanted a route back to her. Nothing about my horrid circumstances resisted that, that's how powerful the feelings were. For reaching anyone, the habit was still ingrained, with or without regular use of the platforms that serve it. It gave me a final hope, although the trip was now over, and the lone flight was putting this dreamlike period to an end. *Was it all a dream?* I couldn't sleep on the flight even if I wanted to. I didn't really know whether it was the uncomfortable seat or something else entirely, but there was a pain flaring up that was different from taking myself away from everything in my life before. Because it wasn't everything. This was something else that came after the day that marked my abandon. I felt like I was excruciatingly pulled away from my core which was left back where I last set my eyes on its fixation in Italy. This wasn't a dream and all the proof I needed for it was my love for this girl. When I got home, the brilliance of the trip didn't stop the pain from consuming me. There was no fairy tale ending to a long, long period of despair. I'd lost it now and the weight of it increased as the jumbo jet flew me further from where it was at the time where love was set. I thought I'd never feel the same again. On top of everything else, the torment included what it was like to have my heart break.

2:7

From this point I was in a critical condition and I blamed myself for absolutely everything. I hated myself. After the trip, I believed that I could never live happily ever after, or anything remotely near to it. My depression became far more aggressive, rushing up from my chest to shriek that I'd met someone who showed a window looking out to happiness, only to see it slammed shut while potentially hurting her too. I made a fragile move to build a bridge to contact her from my final use of the socials. She was from London, an hour's train from me, and our two weeks of having met couldn't quantify the level of feeling that had developed in that short space of time. But it was now so far away. Circumstance commanded that it wasn't to be. Stabs of pain went right into me at every flashback, an agonising picture day and night of the way she looked at me and my failure to meet it. I would punch and scream into my pillow when I woke up, coming to terms with losing the person who had briefly brought me a shimmer of what it was like to feel alive. *Why? Why does this have to happen to me?* An especially melodramatic moment in the shower brought me sliding down in a rain of water as I wept into the pool. Long walks ensued again. This all defined the summer. My phone remained out of sight throughout. I still decided I had to fix up before I could act on the back of that trip. Uni was approaching now, and I'd have to be able to check important emails if I wanted to continue the next three years of my life. I saw that there was a recent flood of unread stuff that reminded me that Facebook updates were always dropping bait on my email. I assumed that the surplus meant that I was in the online group for the tour. The connection was there. All I had to do was log on if I was ready to. The time never looked right, so I never reached out. I struggled to believe that anything I felt was connected with some objective reality. Psychiatric disarray. The decision to wait for whatever was corrosive, but I was certain that nothing could be mended from what was lost from the wounds. I looked at all the dust on the monitor I longed for during school, and it was difficult to take the pain seriously. My mind didn't seem to be resting, but it didn't give my body anywhere to go while it was this lost. Amongst all the throbbing when I lay my head on the pillow, my pain added another dimension with a plague of small, speedy fleas sucking my blood, as sourced by the adoption of a new family kitten whose vet treatment hadn't yet come into effect. As much as I loved raising Pesto, who offered respite at a time of dire need, the awful itching all over my body sent my neural receptors a message of being the finishing touch to the torture. I suppose what I admired about these pesky creatures was that my shaking disbelief of what was happening couldn't quite leave me doubting that they weren't real, although my parent's scepticism of my initial theory of bed bugs hit me while I was unable to work out why my virtual life was so deteriorating to any relationship with any person. Mum asked to see photos from the trip, and complained that I didn't put the effort into getting in contact when I landed abroad. *I'd let everyone down, hadn't I?* I would say I had a lovely time but none of it could make me forget how someone so special had entered my life, only to leave it for the same reason as anyone else on Earth. Picturing the next day never filled me with any kind of excitement. I just wished that I could start again. I'd lost so many good things all over, it was hard to see how I could make anything substantially better. *What was the point?* I was entering uni with an emptiness I failed to see anything filling, and my outward-facing personality was obliterated. *There were only more things to fail.* Life was a defeatist eye searching for an opportunity not to make it any worse. Otherwise, the only thing better appeared to be death.

Part III

3:1

One small block of halls. Around 95 other students. This was in the centre of a campus situated on the outskirts of Brighton, a living arrangement that was going to force me to integrate with human life for at least the next nine months. If I couldn't get back online or carry a phone, at least I was living with a mass of young people under the same roof, however far from my comfort zone sharing the space could be. My malady and I arrived here looking to relearn self-expression, having no idea what other lessons were to come. Rather than live with my parents and continue to be cut off from my generation, I was finding my feet in an environment of diverse individuals to find an identity separate from the tragedy that had previously befallen me. A new life, if I was to call it that, began while I remained offline.

Of course, when any variety of young people are brought together, the socials are the established instrument for aiding togetherness. There was a group chat made for all tenants to make contact before we all moved in. Names apparently popped up with the room number of the person to integrate everyone into a community. A fantastic start. Luckily, when I entered the halls, this didn't prove to be a barrier on the first day. There were so many of us that proper introductions were still to be made. I instantly went from being totally detached from the social world to meeting more people within a few days than I ever had in my whole life. There was no time to think. My room was directly opposite the kitchen I shared with eleven other tenants. The intensity of it all demanded I try. Since I'd gathered little information about the procedure of fresher's week and starting my course, I was grateful that I shared a building with people I could go to lectures with. Security. The first week was a key event, so there was less time for smartphones. There were too many people chatting everywhere. It felt important to get involved, although I was covering up my tele-communicative relationship. I didn't want to embarrass myself here. When walking down the hallway, another new face came out of one of the rooms asking if I had worked out how to get on the campus Wi-Fi.

"Not yet, sorry."

She went back to her room.

For the most part, the first few days were an offline experience but once my senses had taken in much of the new setting, my mind had time to worry about whether I was really fit for uni. Everyone was gathering information straight away on how to enrol as a student and maximise the experience. I had informants, like a residential advisor living in my flat, but it was hard to take a break from the nerves.

I did in fact bring my phone and tablet to uni, but it was kept in a suitcase at the bottom of my bed. Bomb defused. If this was a step to looking after myself better, it didn't change that the behaviour felt irresponsible when it was my first time moving out of home. If I wasn't getting more self-sufficient, I at least found a way to be in a collective. The shared experience in a physical block in the first year at uni made something separate from online validation because we were transitioning into adulthood. The room that was mine was my base position. Our placement in the halls created something deep and meaningful that was new to virtually everyone, and I was comforted at the realization that community wasn't a word that only came from the socials. And because there were people in the block who came internationally or from different places across Britain, people were interested in hearing me talk about Brighton, usually on the topic of its nightlife. Well, incidentally I hadn't been out in Brighton for over a year and I didn't have much of a voice in group planning. I felt myself go red in front of all these party goers, although it was nice that the block opted to spend more time at the student bar on campus so I was new to the village-like setting like them. There were multiple situations to avoid though. When queuing for a free slice of pizza with people, I found at the end of it that I had to engage in some online act with the provider. I pondered for a few seconds how I could get past it this time while standing next to my new mate who got his phone out to perform the requirement. I said I changed my mind and fled. It got increasingly difficult when I had to finish enrolling onto the uni's system. Getting deferred to a senior member of staff for a password issue wasn't a coincidence. I played dumb when I didn't check my email and wanted to get a human being in the room to do it manually for me. A former student instructed me to note down a particular detail and I was wary that there were people waiting behind me to receive help.

"Do you have a pen I could use?" I mumbled.

"Do you have a phone you could use?" they snapped back.

"Erm . . . no."

She walked off to grab a pen. I felt so small. I rushed to get it done and evacuated out of there.

My block was one big party, and my kitchen seemed to be the central spot. Whole evenings were spent there with these new people, with the quirky bar only across the road being another frequent destination. Music, fashion, and current affairs were fed by the other tenants conversing in a way that became a solid source of information in this eventful social environment. When we got a bus into the city together, it felt like a completely different place. *Growing up in Brighton could be dissociated from this new life.*

The walls were very thin in the block, so hearing chatter from my kitchen would often pull me there. I was scarcely mentally prepared after my derailment into isolation, but the content I'd embraced when I did use the socials still rubbed off in relating to other students. The wrong frame of mind didn't stop me referring to jokes and pages with flatmates who'd seen the same, and it became a base for the group's sense of humour. It was years ahead, but a lot of people will never forget the Wealdstone Raider from back in the day. That was one way of acting as one of them, but as people were getting to know each other and became more settled, there were splinters as my practical difference was showing its mark.

"Luke," one flatmate piped up mid-conversation, "When are you going to accept my friend request on Facebook?" He'd found me, and now I had to handle a response to this kind of question in the building where I was living.

3:2

"I've made thirty friends on Facebook in September!" a flatmate exclaimed. Like in the year 7 class, I looked up but didn't answer. I thought into the meaning of what they were saying. This figure could determine how people saw themselves, and my failure in replicating the custom had made me into an uncomfortable rogue. I looked inward, and I saw that I wasn't one of those friends. *I don't have any friends.* I genuinely didn't think I would make any purely because of my relationship with the socials that cast me out of the living world altogether. I told the person who found my profile that I would accept his request. I kept up a lie to people who asked if I was a member of their generation. It felt like the only way to make companionship official so I made promises I couldn't keep. People were different in many ways: socially, cultural, ethnically, and the rest, but the standard for online presence was the same. I was different to the expectation each one of them appeared to carry, and as they established themselves in the block, the coalesced friendliness merged into separate, established groups. My vulnerability was gradually becoming impossible to meander around, so I had to take full advantage of the accommodation being characterised as a walk-in social life where you chat with whoever was around. No matter how unapproachable and subdued I became, the ball got rolling from as little as cooking in the kitchen. Refresh and go. My secret about the socials was commented on before long. What my life had been and how I individually behaved on that basis towards others slowly gained me a reputation within the wider circle. I was the most mysterious one, an enigma. As much as I intended to be honest and loyal in my intentions to form lasting friendships, my incognito status sharply contradicted it. I only wanted to have some close mates again, but this sort of thing disrupted any confidence I tried to recover.

"I still don't know your surname!"

"Everyone wants to know what you're thinking." I was unidentified. The quizzical looks of people passing me in the corridor confirmed my position as an exotic creature that no one could grow familiar with. It wasn't a likely atmosphere to reveal anything personal. The comments got bolder after people had been drinking. It hurt me seeing a bunch of open-minds unready to see a non-digital life. Something must have been very wrong with me. When entering a room full of a large amount of people, someone commented that I should add them so that we could chat. There was a quiet movie night going on with roughly fifteen others. I felt the sideswipe get to me for the rest of the evening, trying to breathe deeply inside my room and understand why this was happening. I became unsure that I was a part of the group on occasions. Again, I blamed myself, being increasingly frustrated that my opportunity to build friendships was in crisis. Even so, I wasn't exactly going to lose touch with them any time soon. I kept on trying. It was the one option other than giving up.

The classes in my course were hard to approach. I could have been missing out on key info that was so easily accessed through the uni's networks. My fundamental source was the voices of other people, whether the tutors, or the three course mates in my flat. The reading lists were online so I didn't spend nearly enough time preparing for seminars whilst trying to wing it by using my past studies. I was getting by to begin with but then two months in, I was asked to submit an essay. It had to be done via a digital word processor which made it automatically problematic. Being very conscious of the change in proportion of notepads to laptops, I had to hope that I was going to be alright soon for the sake of my academic progress. On the last few days before the essay was due in, I had to ask a flatmate if I could borrow their laptop after getting all the reading material from large books where it was hard to narrow down the relevant points for my topic. The face of the situation amused my flatmates. It was a common occurrence for a student to leave it all until the last minute and rush through it – a classic story met with laughter. But in my case, I couldn't reveal how much I was genuinely panicking. Was this what it was like? I would have to improve soon, otherwise I'd be done for, if the assignments were all to be done digitally. Stress.

3:3

Before the first term was up, discussions about housing for second year were happening. Someone had asked me to join them, but it wasn't long before I felt outside the planning process, even after I'd made it clear that I'd rather live in a student house than with my parents. Given my absence from the interactive panel where lives were organised, I took it badly when a potential house was under consideration in talks without me, losing my temper with one of my flatmates who tried to smooth it over with a change of plan. I'd picked up some major trust issues that played into anything people consulted over on the socials. My rejection of my old idea of membership for survival didn't stop me from thinking about the space for organizing that I took no part in. My ultra-sensitive alarm bell was ringing. When talking about the socials, I found that I had become very bitter towards how they were used, but this stance didn't change that I did very much depend on them as I listened closely when friends read out news updates. Not to mention I'd often bring up topics like the football to try and bleed the scores out of other fans without revealing my ignorance on the subject. I detested the socials when I was still young and limited from making sense of why everything happened the way it did. But I couldn't ignore them and I don't think I wanted to. There were always going to be things on them that I would be interested in hearing about, so I used people's attachment to them. I was a second-hand user if it were. There would be no overload on me if it wasn't mine, although I can't deny that I was still dependent.

One evening at the student bar, it was suggested that a few of us play a game where individual players take turns interacting with others in the silly way that was instructed. The game was through a smartphone, and a turn came up saying that all players had to pass their phones to the person on their right and send a message to the last person they had been texting. I froze as everyone thought up what to say.

"Just popping to the loo," I got out of it this time. People got bored and moved on from the round. But when the game was played again a few weeks later, a turn came that was far more direct.

"Ask Luke anything you want to know" someone read from their smartphone.

"Ooh, the power ..." someone quipped.

"Are you a drug dealer?" another blurted out.

The table jeered, "Ah, what a waste of a question!" All but one of them go up to get a round of drinks.

The remaining friend turned to me, "I was going to say, why don't you use social media?" The atmosphere of the game from a bunch of lads in this new environment, coupled with the punching weight of this group interaction brought me to meltdown. It was supposed to be a fun time. I really wanted them to know me so that I could know myself again. Personally, such a casual group interaction merely suggested to me that I was failing to make a comeback, and I was going to have questions consistently aimed at me which I didn't know how to answer. It was always the thing being asked. The talk of me that received the most interest was rooted by the thing I despised the most. I skulked back to the block many times with a mix of anger and hopelessness without letting anyone know about my withdrawal from an event. My motivation sometimes faltered in resuming my reconstruction. I didn't dislike anyone in the block, so I thought I was letting myself down. Entering my accommodation alone at night, there were several times when I yelled out of frustration at the top of my lungs after missing another chance to feel involved. No one was present so the outcry didn't feel real. My mind was disconnected from a world I was desperate to inhabit by force of necessity. But it was that disconnection that invalidated everything I felt in the process. If a tree falls in a forest, but no one is there to hear it, is there a sound? Waking up the next day, I carried on as if it hadn't happened, not knowing how to reflect on it. I didn't see any other option but to continue. The blips didn't stop me travelling the uneven path. Whatever madness that was in there looked to the block to tie it down and steady its host. It didn't feel right to curse society, or some supernatural being, so I kept quiet in between the commotion around me. Life goes on.

3:4

"Have you seen this?"

"Haven't you heard?"

"Do I have you on Facebook?" There was a literal echo of these things spinning and revealing the force that the socials had in grabbing people's attention and therefore themselves. I would lie again. I would try to change the subject. If someone quickly showed me the content of their screen, I would pretend to look at it, fixing my eye on the spot just above where the camera lens is. On one end I couldn't bring myself to look, but I would have felt rude if I put my hand out to push it away. They could dish it out before I had time to say anything. Sometimes, during a party, my flatmate would put their device in my hands to encourage me to select songs for everyone to vibe to. There was little room to manoeuvre. Occasionally, I gingerly accepted before hastily passing it on to someone else. It's all so normal. Saying no all the time was impossible. My Achilles heel was so bizarre, but there it was, in truth, as mysterious to me as to anyone else. Dropping your devices isn't enough to avoid the online world if you're accompanied by people. And I needed people. They were the answer to the question of me being better off dead, if this mess was to threaten everything I tried to apply myself to. Coming clean had to have a balance if everyone visibly used it so naturally. They knew how to live with it, so it was comfortable and I couldn't afford to always defy it if I wanted to move away from all the loss.

Adaptation was hard work, but it was vital. I may have wished to have some injury to give the immediate impression of being hurt from existing besides the socials, but I couldn't make enemies out of people who used them. I wasn't in poverty or a carrier of some deadly disease. I tried to be grateful because activities were happening. It promised good things if I managed to jump the hurdles. I had to be patient. Life is real when its experiences don't always feel so.

The ebb and flow of my mind's hurricane did indeed make me step back a few times to contemplate my sanity. I was among people using devices so central to their way of life, but my own reasoning was insisting that carrying my phone was more harmful than not. Hypochondria wasn't me. I had to make do without it for the sake of my health, even when I was backed into a corner. To turn my phone on because that was the expected way to live would have been more costly than the sense of security for the people who cared.

"We have to be able to contact you ..." but there wouldn't be a positive outcome from phone contact in mental terms. The lights are on but no one's home. I knew what happened next. I was selfish because I was small, but I was also certain that I couldn't physically do it. A lifelong relationship informed me of that. Whatever the extent of my isolation, the selfish part was that I kept it a secret, but no one was dying because I didn't have my phone on. Every obvious benefit of this tool didn't change that I wasn't right to hold it, even if I lost touch with a friend, or couldn't answer calls from Mum to erase her worries. I was nineteen in an online world, with no excuses other than that I wasn't strong and confident enough to request any help to reach what I needed. I branded the problem as me, and only I was in the way of getting past it. I didn't believe that anyone could change but myself, so when I saw an advert for an app called Stay Alive next to the train station, I said I wasn't living so I couldn't install the app to help anyone stay alive, me or anyone else. But when I felt the tension of this off position, I tried to be more reliable in other ways. I wanted to help people feel comfortable while I made myself frequently available for performing favours. I took an interest in improving my athletic ability and understanding how individuals around me organised themselves. It all started on the ground, and I had to evolve if I couldn't use the phone or anything similar. I had to improve at co-existing with others somehow. If my situation was so unique that I didn't think I could tell anyone honestly, then I would listen closely to the quirks of an individual's experiences. No judgement. I knew that differences were there. I'm not the only one. An awareness of these quirks contributes to an awareness of what experiences overlap, and this is taken further by genuinely making someone feel that that there is another person in the world who would give them a full voice in a conversation. It might make someone less of a shadow. There are less parts of them that feel separate from their outwards selves as they become more confident about where they are standing. More things would then be achievable, more problems could be solved, more people would be happy. Anything going on in there doesn't make you a stupid weakling. Anything.

3:5

When I came back from the winter break, there was a letter posted to my room from my flatmate telling me that a bunch were revising for the upcoming exam for our course together. He expressed slight irritation that he couldn't contact me after I gave him my number. We were going to be living together in our second year and he had arranged some house viewings. My new friendships felt like they could switch from heartfelt, to formal acquaintance in an instant, but my carry on and ignore the disgruntlement behaviour eventually amused him. He needed to contact me and I was grateful for the memo. It was also great to revise with my flatmates. One of them would get up practice exam questions from their laptop for us to exchange ideas without me needing to handle anything digital to prepare for a seated paper in a big hall. It was a fair way to get by, but there was also an online hand-in essay. There was no way I could ask my flatmate for his laptop again. I was drawn to the rumour that there was a cluster of computers in a building across from the halls. As it turned out, the public PC limited to my study purposes was safe enough, and I saw it as a future window to work on anything to do with my degree. I was pushed into testing the boundaries, and online functions weren't all outside of them. *Phew.* There were some normal things I could do at last.

Having little say was fine with me. My three future housemates could pick whatever place and bedrooms they liked. I was just thankful that one of them revelled in doing the admin side of it all. Since I was learning to ride the enthusiasm of people sorting out stuff on their virtual space, life seemed to acquire a relative structure. I was thankful that things were getting done. Keep me offline when proceeding forwards, and I will be content. It said to me that I was less alone now anyway. My solo walks to escape were still frequent, but people from the halls exercised with me for fun without needing to phone me. The lonesome activities I associate with my emptiness were now connected with the company of people in the halls. It was a transition that worked wonders in dealing with the pain.

It felt right to knock on doors in the halls. To initiate the social hub from there and gesture towards the next gathering in the kitchen was so simple. It was only down a corridor, but it was a profound act that got me into a life with people again. I'd forgotten what kind of impact this can have on one's mental health. Talking about a passion for hours with someone was something every human needed to do from time to time for the sake of simply sharing your passion with another mind. It was sad to admit that I didn't branch out much from the halls, unless other tenants were bringing in people they knew. But the intensity of the social space helped me learn to cooperate with every kind of different personality, even when one or two people were getting on my nerves. Of course, I didn't have the power or mobility to organise much of a social meeting in advance on my own, so I had to remain civil regardless of my flatmates turning the volume up to eleven on a night before I had to get up early for work. The halls were all I had. My ghostly status couldn't bar me from bonding over being under the same roof. In this style of commune, it was appropriate for anyone to slot in if they worked hard enough and didn't consistently bother anyone. The off comment of someone not knowing me who'd lived close by for over six months usually nudged another to show some extra compassion. We were all encountering sides to people we hadn't seen before. Education wasn't merely academic at uni. But my new friends didn't acknowledge that my zero response to friend requests meant that I was offline. Some of them interpreted that I wasn't including them in my profile and found it slightly offensive.

"Surely, he does but he's keeping it tucked away from us." Without me communicating any sign of reason to them, they seriously thought that there was an unwillingness on my part to represent any association with them. Two of my newly assigned housemates approached me in the student bar when I was looking morose.

"You don't need to have everyone on it. You can just add the two of us and make do with that," one of them assured me. They knew by now that there was a deep sadness in me. The socials were where people looked to boost their mental health and people expected others to do so. I looked up at them with what must have struck them as a pained expression. These two pals would take time out of a party to steady me with both hands if they saw me begin to wobble, but my black dog was a completely different breed to the one they thought they saw. The least I could do was promise them that it wasn't anyone else's behaviour at uni that stopped me from letting any of the block into my virtual space. That was the most truth I could bring out. But people seemed to be uncertain. If you can't exchange online accounts, then a connection between individuals isn't as confident. I didn't do that ordinary thing of popping up on their screen to organise and secure whatever they were meaning to do. And there were some egos who didn't like it either.

"You're a bit stuck up," I heard across the table. There was little I could do, and it all added up. Pushing away from online activity was read as pushing real people away too, and it wasn't a demeanour that made it feel safe to speak up on something so conflicting to their way of life.

"We'll loosen you up next year, Luke. I think we're going to become firm friends," my third future housemate said to me. I smiled and nodded, but I also felt something funny in my gut. It was the online world I didn't trust, not them. That's not the same thing, surely? Time didn't seem to be slicing this barrier away. *Are they my friends?* All these different people shared a curiosity in the mystery man, although they didn't doubt that I owned a phone.

"I have never seen your phone," one declared in the kitchen. I guessed it wouldn't have passed unnoticed in a shared living space for nine months. A few days later, when it was only us two in there, I grabbed my phone out of my pocket (switched off), ready to fend off the encroaching investigation, pretending to swipe on something on the screen while he was facing my direction from the other end of the room. It was intended to be a brief spectacle from a distance of a few meters. I wanted to reduce the chance that he'd call me out in front of more people next time. It was a matter of self-preservation.

3:6

One day, I woke up with a stomach bug, and decided not to get up and leave my room. Today, my pattern of constantly wanting company was suspended. I vacated because I didn't want to face anyone. The next bout left me thinking that I was sick and tired of the shortfalls of my rehabilitation. My bedroom door was locked; curtains drawn shut. I curled up and remained still, dwelling on another uncomfortable evening trying to integrate. All it took to tip me over was a belly ache. *What am I doing?* People in the halls had made a conscious effort to be welcoming towards me, only to be left unsatisfied. I thought that they had given up on me. *What am I going to do?* Going outside wouldn't make me feel like I was doing anything. I didn't want to be seen, and going to my parents saying I wanted to do overtime at work was a card I'd played too often by now. I was done with working out another way. I stopped eating and washing myself – habits I'd never given up before. There were several knocks on the door throughout the day. After one of them, there was a pull on the door handle that made me panic. I didn't hear any voices. This was a very different space to the corridor outside. I didn't consider how well-meaning these spells of attention were. I was telling myself I couldn't do it. Everything was failing, so now I wished the rest of my internal system to do the same. The fire was finished. I was burnt out, having been in the halls for over half a year and gathering more reasons to think that I'd let everyone down again. Same thing, different day, everywhere I go. *There's no one in here.* Whatever this bond was with the halls, it only made me feel the gravity of being immensely incapable of being in a room full of people and getting involved in something real. If being offline in a non-comprehensive way was a barrier to taking part, then there was nothing to gain that amounts to more than any loss I've felt before it. All except pain. The knocking was only another invitation to it.

3:7

"Haven't seen him in two days."

"Maybe he's gone to his parents."

"No, he would have said."

"He always goes in the kitchen so I have no idea where he is." There was urgent knocking on the door.

"Luke! Are you in there?"

After a pause, the door handle turned. More knocking. In fairness, I hadn't left my room for more than a day, but I'd vanished before for a couple weeks before term started, so it was a bit strange that someone sensed this time was different. There were multiple voices out there, and a debate ensued on whether the security reception should be called to get someone to come and open my door. It was voted in favour. The voices were fading in the hallway.

"What is it!?" my voice cracked. My panic attack increased in magnitude. This kind of drama was too much for me to continue laying there. I darted out of my bed and opened the door into the blinding lights.

"What's going on?" I called towards the back of the last person. They turned in astonishment and then called to the others. The stage-fright hit me as they asked about my wellbeing. My eyes had barely adjusted to the light. I had no time to appreciate their concern, going from being locked in my room to nervously saying that I was okay in front of a crowd of people. It felt like it had been two months since I'd seen them, the halls were that intense, but the gestures of these people put the equilibrium of despair on hold. It increased the brightness to a better level, even if it could become overwhelming. I preferred the uncomfortable intensity to the horrific place where nothing decent would come if I didn't rise to want the next day to be better than the last. I'd just been pushed out of that. I struggled to let them but they managed it, and I felt better for it in the meantime. Sometimes, a bit of a nudge might be necessary. This was the reality of a support network that didn't clash with a social code that I was the other to. They took time out of their day to come and ask if I was okay. That bit of humanity beckoned me to continue. Not being shy to ask that question can make someone more okay than how they were in that lonely headspace only moments before. When someone asked me if I was living in the Stone Age when trying to organise something, it didn't change that I needed the rendezvous. My head wasn't living in the Stone Age, because I was going to meet up with him in 2018. These halls were the site to learn how to team up with abnormality, for anyone as much as me.

After getting the bus into town one evening, I went up to the entrance to a bar before remembering that I hadn't brought my ID, a laughable error. I was in pretty good form with the group this time, so I told them that I was going to make the six-mile journey to campus and back. Although they said they were going to be in the same place, one of them got their phone out in a flash and tried to hand it to me to add my number to assure him that I'd come back by being on his official list of friends. I replied that I'd see him in an hour and turned away. My mentality was that the connection to this embryonic circle depended on doing the journey back and forth as quickly as possible. The buses were infrequent so I ran the distance and later witnessed everyone's surprise after they thought my night was over. I told myself I needed it and the extreme length to keep the momentum going was more stable than the bitter equilibrium of withdrawal. Today was not the day to let a little mistake disconnect me more. Dropping my past online activity didn't change me from wanting to feel connected in my non-digital status. The near sprint was evidence of that coming into motion to intervene in the gap between living socially and living with online profiles. Offline connectivity became my own invented necessity when I discovered how life-affirming its results were. It was great fitness too.

My parents didn't have a big online presence through the smartphone before I entered my twenties. Dad didn't even use a smartphone, on principle. He regularly complained about people on their phones and not looking where they were going in busy public places, and said he didn't want to be a zombie. His pay-as-you-go, brick, burner phone, was his tool of choice – mobile communication stripped back from entertainment to utility. Mum on the other hand did use it more towards the socials end of the spectrum. It was a feedback mechanism of interests in her wider world that was referenced from her phone. Neither of them barely added to the pressure of connecting as such however, while I was surprised to hear that some of my friends had their folks on the socials. I never had, but since moving away from them, the question of being reachable came more directly as the updates I couldn't receive in my weekly stop after work weren't coming from the missed calls and unanswered texts.

"Did you get my message?" Mum asked.

"Yeah," I lied. Getting caught out didn't stop me. "I am using my phone, Mum! Sorry I missed your message. What did you want to tell me?" Every time, I dodged the questions, and if my parents pointed to the moral side, I put it back on them.

"We need to be able to contact you, Luke. What if something happened?" Mum added. Anything was used to escape the subject of my personal taboo. Getting to the truth would be impossible if I faked it in my mind before an enquiry ensued. The secret was safe because I knew it was all in my head. I was ashamed to reveal any of the invisible fire in there. Besides, avoiding the subject usually supplanted the memory of when it all began anyway. Considering how long ago that was, that part was easy. Meanwhile the fight went on, every second of every day.

3:8

Time was ticking. Before bed I would look at a university wall calendar pinned up in my room. Working out how long I had until the tenancy ended, my faith in time to heal my wounds was dithering as the months went by. This really hit me during the winter when there was a series of strikes at uni. People got bored. I could do extra shifts, or exercise, but my personal progression was centred on hanging out with real people. By now it was clear that it was the strongest shelter from the trauma and pain from losing my social life once before. Me-time was unfavourable when my feeling of uncomfortable restraint didn't get me severely anxious about the idea of doing something wrong in front of someone. I fell short of including myself because I worried about it leading to the pressure of the socials or the phone. I wondered what was going to happen to me. To go into adulthood with this arresting issue of being non-contactable would inevitably clash with ordinary practice. I was frightened. Why was a problem born at a different time still at large? Could I really live with it much longer? Telecommunication was the way of life, the socials added to the reasons for its purpose. It all established how people connected, and fizzled out any other mode in their mind that was around before its fruition. There was very abstract tension between my mind and others, and the thought of that was ammunition alone to the bombardment of my self-esteem when I wanted most of all for positive relationships to last. All of this was going on while my tools were kept under my bed, while I followed the next person's life when the full extent of my reach to anyone was limited without the seemingly unlimited catalogue of data and people. If I was seen to be taking no part by people who cooperated through it, then I wasn't cooperating. Therefore, I was suspect. I could have been a bad person who couldn't be trusted, a delinquent from the place that makes everyone's life convenient. I was incapable of giving an answer to the enigma I had become. I didn't think that telling a flatmate that I was unwell would qualify for one. It discounted the bond. I wasn't protected when the party was disappointed with the show. What was I thinking? *I needed you but I wished I was adequate to fully integrate without the stigma attached.* There was a running joke made about me being an assassin or secret agent who was in hiding. A snigger here and there came about when one muttered to a neighbour round the table that I could have murdered someone. I was way too unstable to take it lightly every time. If all these young people truly perceived conventional contact as the definition of being a legitimate member of society, then I didn't tick that box as well as many others. *Where could I go? Where's left to stand?* I couldn't be alone again, but neither could I get on board with the ways people identified with one another. I evacuated from social evenings if these thoughts pressed down too hard, although I always had a reset in mind. *Rehab isn't working today, let's walk out the door again.* Sometimes that was just a part of the cycle. But why were the same feelings still flaring up after people had literally opted to go to security to check on me? *I could walk back into the social circle but why wasn't all of me really getting there? Such a trap. I am my own worst enemy wherever I go. This is a totally different place with so many opportunities, and I still can't beat the same problem.*

Evacuating out the block again, I walked straight towards the woods outside campus to prepare to give up for the last time. Directing down the woodland path deep into the expansive park, my thoughts went to the girl I fell deeply for in Italy. *What would she think of this? What would she do here?* My memory of her winning smile felt like a dream, as I tried to picture her eyes looking into mine on that glowing street in Florence, from where she radiated. *Such a warm place, although none of it changed that everything missed its mark.* All the chances I had of having a good thing going felt like they'd moved on, and my heart deeply sunk at the thought that for all those things to go wrong, I must have been in an irreparable condition. It's not every day that I could run for miles to save my skin. The grand total of days that represent my malady's life span told me that if I was so bad that all the golden moments didn't result in what naturally should have happened at the end of them, then anything else that came into my life would pass and go, giving me layer upon layer of unspeakable suffering. I stopped on the path. It was sundown on a Friday evening and I was getting cold and hungry, having no clue how long I'd been walking. My hand whipped out a coin. Heads or tails? *Life or death.* The coin flipped and landed on my palm. There was no wildlife in sight to remind me of the grounding influence of nature's movements. It was getting darker. The shadows beneath the trees were starting to take a more prominent shape as the bright greenery faded from my eyesight. I didn't want to open the palm of my hand. A violent shiver hit me from the cold. People tend to feel that way when they are in the woods at night in winter. That can be responded to just like any other effect that reaches you. For all their power, the socials won't change that. I put the coin in my pocket and went back to find my friends again. There's a bit inside me that kept telling me to do that. Locked in my room, out in the woods, or a couple of steps away from being smashed by a lorry, that part of me spoke out when it felt like there was nothing else in there to listen to it. I was glad that part wasn't lost yet, the grand champ of my system when it felt the chronic breakdown topple down everything else that I'd ever loved.

3:9

Not being limited to instant messengers, young people around me used the socials to emit a projection of themselves and what they were up to. This is where people relate to anything coming from what they curate. It also meant that you don't have to use teletext to be certain of the time. The updates and interactions provoke the topic of conversation, stimulating the consumption of trends for a sociable purpose first and foremost. The memes are ready to deploy. Some of them everyone knows. They could be around forever if they stick out enough. I referenced them to add to commentaries of shared situations even after I was no longer directly consuming online content for myself. We imitate behaviours and apply them somewhere else, mostly to see the funny side of something, but always to produce an air of membership over to anyone close enough to receive the transition of the copy. It's the effect of them that can make a real-life experience feel important. The deft device in people's pockets can influence the kind of language they speak; a real-life scenario is tagged with the online-led phrases to bring an everyday situation to the attention of anyone else who sees you.

The mobile phone is called the phone. The phone doesn't refer to a landline but a mobile phone. A smartphone can get picked up without thinking, the impulse prompts the action, the electronic page is read, the hardware is subliminal to the material it provides for our curiosities that clasp it to the mind. It becomes more intimate than the physical device held next to our bodies or sat in our primary bags. I would have probably noticed someone unfollowing me on Instagram before a new crack on my screen. Sat in the kitchen with a flatmate, it went quiet for only a second before their phone was out for a swipe to satisfy the craving to make a fill of gratification. The back of their mind knows that it would feel good to pour something fresh into the space it so smoothly attends. Is it possible to live without it after giving so big a role? That question troubled me when I put it away. Giving life and stealing from it had never been so juxtaposed.

A takeaway delivered for a bunch of us came from a friend's phone. The labour put into shopping couldn't be saved by making an order. I couldn't facilitate a supply chain to gather food or things I couldn't find in town. When alone, my buying habits were often more inconvenient as I missed out on the methods of possession in the mainstream sense. And if I did chip in for a takeaway with my mates, I had to make a mental note of the money to return in cash. Maybe it was easier to pay for something that they wanted from the shop. It's normally customary to bank transfer, but I still took the opportunity to get involved in a shared activity, even if it bred a bit of confusion to begin with.

"Wait, let's work this out." I felt a pang of guilt for adding difficulty or mental effort for others. This took a bigger step when I had to sign an online contract for the tenancy in my second year. My three housemates kept asking if I'd done it after reminder emails were rolling in from the letting agent. There was also a group project on my course that required organization with other students. Out of the 150 students on the course, I couldn't tell who was initially in my group and there were less loopholes here. I wasn't facing the music but my do it tomorrow attitude doesn't change the deadlines. Sleep was lost as the desperation heightened. I was tempted to plead with my course mate in the halls to log in and do the admin for me but I thought the request would make him uncomfortable. I felt the walls closing in on me. It was never easy to borrow a laptop and quickly do it but hey, I scraped by, although the stress convinced me that the next time might give me a heart attack. I cherished the relief and fresh air afterwards. I went out for a run after that experience on the tight rope.

I must have looked like a deer in the headlights, although it's not every day that an old school friend bellows at you in a busy shopping centre.

"Oh my (So and So). Everyone thought you were dead!" He was in the company of someone I went to college with who performed the social cue after witnessing the behaviour of my friend. We briefly caught up as my old world came full force into my face again to the point where it was difficult to talk about what I had been going on for the last eighteen months. When we parted ways, my expectation of what would happen next became a reality.

"Get on Facebook," he said finally, without saying anything more about where the friendship would play out next. No plans on the spot or ideas for rekindling. Connectivity called, and I didn't see this member again.

3:10

Dropping off laundry at home in the typical student manner, I saw Mum about an hour before I had work. She said she'd tried to contact me, but didn't press it in the same way as usual. Instead, she asked me to sit down. At first, I thought I was about to be in big trouble, as I've always been on edge about what's to come when I open the front door. But before she finished, I broke down in tears. Grandpa was on his deathbed, and it was a matter of hours before he was gone.

"Do you want to take the day off work?" Mum asked. I was in no state to break my barrier to phone in so I chose to go in and face the day on top of this news. It would be easier than overcoming my dilemma there and then. I never pulled a sicky, being more comfortable turning up on the odd occasion when I was feeling a bit rough. This time was the same, but the thought of my family being unable to reach me when my grandfather was dying sent a shiver down my spine. I was unable to make complete sense of my problem with the phone, and that fact was a source of my fear and the plummeting of my self-worth when the moral side of ill contact slapped me in the face. But this wasn't about me. Mum's dad was passing away. I was the eldest grandchild of four with the other three being children. When Mum drove me to Grandma's the next day to get together with all the family, I knew I couldn't spend the day in my shell. There needed to be solidarity out in the open.

Coming towards the end of the halls and my assessments, time seemed to be picking up some serious speed. I didn't know what a long summer break would do to the relations with all my flatmates. If I got too close, would it only bring people disappointment? They would inevitably ask how to contact me. The bond I had with these people urged me to try and prove how much they meant to me. On the final night, I tried to console my mate who didn't get their ideal house set up for the next year, telling him that he was welcome at mine whenever he needed. This reassurance led him to ask how he could contact me over the summer. I made a promise I couldn't keep when I didn't want to let him down at the time. I worried what three months would do, but some of my friends were going to be living with me for at least another year. Regression won't change that fact.

"Come to London," were the last words another housemate said to me. He'd been saying it for a while, believing that I'd get on well with his friends there, but regardless of my deeper interests, my disconnected life had always prevented me from making the trip. I nodded back to him and reflected on all the things I'd said that I couldn't live up to. I complied with the sentiments expressed at the end of our first year, begging myself to be more consistent during the next. Throughout the troughs I'd endured since becoming a fresher, I hadn't recovered the memory of being able to sit and think to myself that I was fine, but these people were opening me up to a life that I could grow into besides the predisposed wasteland of my mental state. I've had some fun as a young person in today's age. I was given a face at times, when there was nothing there that I could see in the darkness born before it. I put everything into working on that more. I exited the halls without contact details, saying no proper goodbyes in fear of seeing disappointed faces. Time to disappear again, but not for too long.

Part IV

4:1

It was going to get worse before it got better. The hubbub of campus life in the first year fizzled out so everything slowed down again. I was back home and the bottle neck thinned to the point where there was little to take my mind off the spontaneity of feeling suicidally ill. It was good to have the garden centre as a secure safety net when my idea of personal progression would have otherwise been endangered. Sometimes doing six days a week, saving money became the goal of the summer. The idea of getting another job was unthinkable while I was still digitally outcast in a way that couldn't be accounted for. I tried not to undermine the net if it got tedious. Two months to get through before I got my shared household, and the quiet after such an intense first year made it easy for my internal dialogue to steer away from the thick of something great, to reaching here: the same old place again. All of it was an unspoken experience. On a train back from a day out with Mum, it got tense as we talked about the subject of being contactable. Pointing my finger back at her with rage, it got heated in public when she attempted to get to the truth. I'd already tried to storm off earlier in the day.

"What's going on!?" she demanded. My fury in reaction made

her later contemplate if she was a bad mother. I disagreed again, but this time it wasn't in a defensive, prickly way. It was the guilt that made me cool down and try to reassure her as we sat on a seaside bench. But again, on the train back, I didn't break.

"Whatever it is, I'll sort it, so tell me," she said, in a way that reached towards my innermost self. The power of it didn't change anything. The real-life implications of my cyber-relations were something I didn't consider anybody could relate to, in or out of my generation. While my conditions appeared decent, I suppose that semblance was integral to the peril. You couldn't see the damage. I wasn't shouting nonsense, or behaving in any way that pertains to madness (maybe). So, in theory, I should have been fine. But I really wasn't. *Why do I feel worse inside when someone gets the impression that I've got it all together? Was I acting all the time? Who am I? What's happening to me?* I cried myself to sleep, relegated by all the shame of feeling so different to what appeared on the surface. I thought about the sort of grime you find at the bottom of a gutter. Any loss of equality provided was my own doing, and my failure to connect the dots between the socials and how I felt made me wish to have anyone else's problems, whatever they were. I begged to find more simplicity in mine, wishing to find a solution as I stroked my cat after waking up in the morning. Pesto has such a simple life, not venturing outdoors into a world whose complexities often have cruel ends. Why couldn't I just be Pesto? Then it would be fine. Eat, sleep, get affection, then dash up and down the stairs, whacking the scrunched-up paper, like the wild animal he is. It looked like a great time.

As soon as the day arrived when I had access to my student house in the city, I entered, having no idea when the other three would do the same. I was more nervous than excited about the next step: a house and a year that counted towards the final grade of my degree. I wondered how much contact everyone was having during the summer, stressing over whether I could catch up against the assumption that everyone knew everything while I was out of the loop. Paranoia became a byword for it. I had no idea when my old flatmates were moving into the city. Estimations were limited to late summer unless contact resumed any earlier. When I stopped by a few days later, there were things strewn in the front room. There were the sounds of footsteps coming down the stairs and my university bubble opened again. It took some time to adjust and have my youthful side come out to enjoy things. The separation anxiety felt ridiculous by the time I left the house.

My housemate said that there was a plan to meet a couple of others later, so I sheepishly said I'd see him back at home without any mention of telecommunication. When I came back, he was nowhere to be seen. I imagined him deliberately leaving earlier than stated so that I'd have to phone him to get involved, a ruse to get my phone which he knew his number was on with its missed calls. He wasn't seen for a few days and I never pressed to find out.

I hadn't known they'd all moved in. I was half a mile away but when I did the final round of bringing my stuff over, it all began again. Other friends from the halls were coming in too. These points of contact made my attempt at a social life start motoring again.

"Oh, and Luke by the way... there's a party coming up and they said at the bottom of the group: 'And someone invite Luke'." If the gesture was somewhat uncomfortable, it also hit me that it was coming from a friendly place. The practical circumstances had become common knowledge, so it was a base to springboard from if I wanted to put my public withdrawal to a close.

My friends saw how I engaged with the circle they knew was important to me, and they worked with it more than before. We were all in proximity for the next year, despite no longer living under one roof. Phone or no phone, we were all in this together and I was boosted from a lifeline existing with this kind of familial sentiment. Like the first year, our open plan living area was the social hub, a spirit lifting setup that I'd pay the price of a messy communal space to have it help on my off days. The locale distributed my friends so that I could bump into them without needing to organise anything with a phone. It was the healthiest thing my inner needs could be answered to. The stabilization effect was a saviour, but I wasn't out of the dirt yet. Some of the hottest heads continued to make digs as if I was challenging the rules of life. Beliefs were frustrated by the conflict my circumstances posed, and it became harder to bite my tongue. Uni was a place to explore all kinds of ideas through debates, but sometimes people's passions brought out comments as soon as alcohol gets consumed. You weren't a proper living person without your phone, and that message coming from someone I respected was enough to make me sneak out of the vicinity. If I was less distressed about doing music on a friend's phone for the room, or doing a silly selfie to play out the irony when the owner wasn't looking, it didn't change that I was toying with a separate world that I was far from alright to re-enter. And one time, I was thrown off when my housemate's girlfriend saw me pick up his phone.

"What are you doing?" she asked suspiciously. She didn't get the jest that the one without the phone was taking a pic of himself on his mate's. I was never going to glance at texts, being far less than interested. Yes, I was subconsciously testing my boundaries. I knew the phone's owner would have liked it but the mystery man brought out people's social anxieties, and as a depressive I detested it.

4:2

Board games at uni were brilliant. Rather than spend excessive time in our respective bedrooms, me and my housemates would sit in the front room, playing long interactive sessions that were a lot of fun when we were staying indoors. We often had friends over to unleash everyone's competitive side while also having a laugh in a predominantly offline room. I couldn't have asked for a better pastime. There were no socials (mostly), just a bunch of us in the room enjoying some childhood nostalgia or learning something totally new – a stress relief from the week's challenges, while parts of the evening were about talking about that too. I was over the moon that people in their twenties still loved a board game and picked it over the easy entertainment on their phone or computer.

The deadlines of the first term that corresponded with my final degree had mostly been exam papers after the winter break. All my notes were on paper compared to most people's laptop word processors so I was effectively studying without any topped-up stress from online learning. Three out of four times, I was in a pressured environment of a big sport hall sitting down and writing on question papers, like all the traditional exams in school. I think I was in the minority of people who felt more comfortable being assessed in this way. Indeed, I had a sense that I could study physical books better than webpages, processing significant information in a more scholarly way than retreating to direct quotes from an academic article. Naturally, I learnt more when I wasn't straining through the blue light that slightly reminded me of my life's turmoil. The results from the exams turned out to be more than the best I hoped for. I almost leapt in delight inside the library after nervously looking them up on one of the PCs. It was funny because the evening before I went into one of the exams, I sliced a deep cut on the tip of the middle finger of my writing hand after prying open a tin-can of food. The following hour's gush of crimson and light-headedness was inferior to the unrelenting pain the next day of squiggling in the exam hall with a gaping wound beneath my wraps of bandage. I don't know whether it was a good omen, but I couldn't help but wonder that my peculiar malaise was a far more formidable disadvantage than the struggle to keep up a pace of writing in under two hours with an excruciating throb against my pen. Another exam, too soon before I could heal, saw a similar result. All the online assessments for the rest of my degree wouldn't match them. What a coincidence! Dare I say my learning experience was far richer off the digital platforms. Surely, I'm hinting at a conspiracy, aren't I? Or perhaps I was getting to know how I worked more productively.

When it comes to parties, it's a given that people make the extra effort to dress up to be seen and have photos taken for a performance encounter in adolescent life. One day, my housemate told me that someone who had lived with us in the halls had made a group on the socials for a house party. I didn't know them very well at the time, but apparently they tried to find me on Facebook by looking at the friends list of my housemate to invite a different Luke on there who wasn't even living in the same city. The host hadn't realised that I wasn't on the socials, and when she accidently added another individual, I burst out laughing with my hostility to online life. On another occasion at a group meal, there were eyebrows raised as to how I knew about what was going on after I arrived there like everyone else. Someone at the table joked that one day I would accept their friend request on Facebook, as if to address an incompleteness to the friendship. Even if I reacted humorously, it still contributed to my overall insecurity of how strong a bond really could be without making up a number on a list of friends. Hey, you couldn't ring me but if we arranged then I wouldn't use a bad reason to let you down. I didn't have the ease of saying I can't make it simply because I couldn't be bothered in the moment. The process weighed more when it wasn't so easy to cancel. There's no knowing how that might be received on the other end, so if they're having a good or bad day, I'd rather be there for them than sit in my bed watching Netflix. My virtual non-existence changed what friendship meant to me.

I sighed.

"What's up?" my housemate asked.

"Nothing," I muttered. There was so much I couldn't do. There were days when I couldn't reach any authentic recourse without dreading an online booking before saying yes to do something in the outside world. I didn't know what to say. A paralysis contained me as I failed to explain the source. The secret to this long-run conflict with connectivity was not something I could connect to the unshakable discontent in my twenty-year-old mind that friends were seeing. It was tiring work getting my mood to their level, when I wasn't coordinating a lot of things for myself. Sometimes the apathy got the better of me, making it impossible to appreciate the things that I had. I should have been grateful for the joyous spontaneity of my energetic friend bursting in on a Friday evening, demanding me to get excited for the weekend. But one thing that broke the deadlock for a time in the January break between those finger-throbbing exams and the new term starting was an idea put ahead by my housemate and fellow history enthusiast.

"Luke... do you fancy a trip to Chernobyl this month?" All the online parts, booking flights, accommodation in Kiev, and a tour of the perimeter of the nuclear disaster zone, had been done for me. I didn't need a device to transfer the money I owed to him. Luckily the bank still carried that function in branch once my mate had written down his details for me. I'd known so much nothingness, having so little cheery stories to tell at the pub to a bunch of students. Now, me and eight others were going on a lads' holiday to Chernobyl in the bleak midwinter. As we showed our boarding passes to the airline staff members, the look of bewilderment on their faces was an absolute picture I could never forget.

4:3

I was looked after and never on my own. Maps were out and we found the places we needed to get to. My second-hand smartphone usage got me through an unfamiliar place to see landmarks, exchange currency, and locate the accommodation. We roamed around the Ukrainian capital and were then led by an eccentric tour guide within the site of the biggest nuclear accident to date. The inhabitants of the nearby town of Pripyat didn't have the socials to alert one another and spread information about the scene in 1986 while Premier Gorbachev did everything in his power to leave the event unreported. I knew what it was like to live in the unknown, but people living here were in grave danger as they remained unaware of the scale of the radioactive meltdown. How times have changed for reporting news of this type. Communication and information determine where life leads you. Visiting Chernobyl made me very conscious of some of the subtler effects of how I'm connected with the world, since most of what I hear comes from the mouths of people.

The trip ended with my friends downloading their boarding passes at the airport, which made my dependency on them as clear as day. It cost extra to get it printed at the reception desk of the terminal. My slightly irritated housemate led the way, giving me that familiar feeling of isolation when this kind of admin was swiftly conducted on the smartphone while my mate held the proof I needed. Slightly embarrassing. All I could do was silently proceed while I looked very backward in public. I must have belonged to a different age for navigation and travel. Paper maps and travel agents at a desk were always nice.

I lost count of the number of times I'd felt like I was making up for the countless interactions being missed online. I thought chatting had to be substantial in person to maintain the friendships

I found in the halls. Wherever they were, they were in contact, while I must have come across as patchy and unpredictable. I shouldn't have been surprised about a person quickly gaining a significant place in someone's life without seeing one another for a while. I met people whom I clicked with on my course, but sadly chance had made the connection die fast because I couldn't point it to a medium of contact. There were others for them to meet and add on the socials to see again while I faded out of their life as quickly as I'd entered it. There's no telling how different my life would have been. We all lose people we like, but the relative extent in the offline life felt seismic in a way I struggled to come to terms with.

I could also clearly see that romance was put into motion through virtual contact. All three of my housemates were in a relationship, and their girlfriends were frequently round when we had our evening board games sessions. The practical boundaries alone informed me that I was foolish to try, so when there was pressure to talk to someone, I found it quite suffocating. The socials were the catalyst, without them everything in that department felt terrifyingly out of reach. People didn't see that side of me, and the lack of it didn't pass unnoticed. Many comments poured out when they were a bit intoxicated.

"You got your eyes on anyone?" Men particularly were forming some very far-fetched conclusions about me. Someone went as far as asking me in a group setting if I had been married before. A young student in a very sociable environment couldn't get away from it. It's what people think about, but with me it stopped from there before my ingrained inferiority complex started telling me that I wasn't good enough anyway. My housemate's girlfriend asked me if I felt left out as the only single person living in the house. I didn't really know the answer to that question, and the zero clarity brought me lower into the muddy trench I thought I already knew too well. If my intrusive thoughts were put on hold enough to talk to someone for a little while then some of my friend's faces appeared to be hit by a stun grenade. No masculine pressure was going to change anything though, it didn't matter what type of tequila they bought me at the bar, my pre-emptive restraint had a much stronger influence. Rightly or wrongly, I believed that being phoneless was going to make someone look elsewhere in the dating world, and no one was going to make me have a device in my pocket. Time had already told that. An old flatmate remarked that my relationship with technology resembled something like his grandad's. I would have betted that I used devices far less.

"You know... she only lives around the corner, Luke." I imagined knocking on someone's door and making them uncomfortable as they answer this big move. Either that or a giggling housemate. People organise their dating life online because they can chop and change the encounter without fear of embarrassment or having to initiate difficult interactions face to face. The only time I did feel left out was Valentine's Day. Always full of abstract pressure, my housemates planned a triple date and accepting the seventh seat would have really dragged me down. But when my other friends brought up the idea of four single lads going bowling together, my depression slipped away for an evening as I knocked on their door and forgot about it all for the next few hours. Against the odds, it was the best Valentine's Day I'd ever had, being the opposite to the bravado coming in every weekend as my housemates made out that I had to go for this person or I'd let myself down. Sorry I didn't ask for their number. There was no pen or paper nearby.

4:4

A rather unique social event was coming up that everyone was going to be attending. My friends were organizing a Masquerade Ball for students, and while my housemate was one of the planners, and had my ticket, my anxiety didn't dim around the e-ticket process. How daft was that?

"I've got your ticket here, Luke," I was told at the door. The lack of visible proof made me worry, regardless of who was in charge. I would have felt bad asking them about it before that night because they were busy trying to sort out their first event as aspiring organisers while I was the only one having this technical difficulty. Silly me. Once my tension loosened up, the event turned out to be a watershed for breaking out of being camera shy. The attire was very different from the usual uni party, being for a ball where you had to wear masks. Such an aesthetic helped me embrace the occasion, and I was walking up and saying hello to everybody. The pretended disguise cancelled my perception of myself as a nobody. You're supposed to be mysterious with Masquerade. I was well attuned and ready for it on that basis. The whole idea was to let loose of the usual boundaries while the tradition covered the associations people entrench via the socials too. It didn't matter, and I felt a lot freer because of it, jumping into camera shots in a way I hadn't done for years. I probably featured in more photos on the online event page than I had in the rest of uni before it. It only took a plastic mask from a tradition born long before the socials.

I felt my relative comfort zone expand from the bottleneck when I was happy to join in with calls on loudspeaker between my housemates and other friends. Talk of going for a kickabout made me pipe up with enthusiasm. It wasn't a smartphone I had responsibility for, so I could push back what may have once triggered any bad memories. Also, since music was consumed online, I was delighted when my housemate made a playlist featuring different songs both of us loved. My offline life had some indirect exemptions without all the words, pictures, and videos affecting how I felt. I was able to convince myself that my issue wasn't just my head being situated in Cloud Cuckoo Land. Word had spread about my offline status, but when someone said that they wished they could do the same, it left me totally bewildered.

"I bare rate that!" another commented. I didn't know what to say. The opinions of students on my grand harbour of disgrace left me baffled when a portion of them considered it a pass for respect. They claimed that they desired a bit of the same, but didn't think that they could perform it. It was the direct opposite to what was going through my head. I hated the online world's role in my life, but I wished I didn't have to make it defunct and run away from everything. I still felt it was necessary for my life to function. I never expected the only path to my survival to be in the same sentence as 'edgy', so I almost wanted to ask if they fancied a life swap. On the other hand, I got the sense that these interactions were covering more than simply finding it cool. People were talking about their mental health in a variety of ways in relation to how they felt about their activity on the socials, and a lot of the time it wasn't all good things. There's more to it than fake news or cyberbullying. There was a complexity to it like the conversation on how to better cope with our thoughts and feelings altogether.

4:5

My social anxiety got more imposing after moving back to Brighton. The chance of bumping into old faces could seize me up, in a city small enough for it to happen. Identifying two old friends coming towards me from a distance, I made a lap around the streets to avoid them before they passed, on a cold Sunday evening when I needed to wait for the bus. I was on high alert when alone, and seeing a part of the world where I failed to feel good swoop back in, it put my disconnection from virtual reality straight into my face. I held no grudges against anyone, but the collision was unwelcome when I watched it coming without me having a shield against the ensuing panic that came from my anticipation of a weak explanation about my disappearance. It could make saying hello to someone one of the hardest things in the world. *What did they think of me?* I had no pole of identity to retreat to. My precarious offline position felt forever exposed. Choice felt subordinate to the flicker of hope in waiting for the burning ruins of my mind to extinguish and leave room for reconstruction. I was jumpy when encounters came out of the blue. A honk from a friend's car must have made me look like I'd leaped out of my skin before I quickly composed myself for a chat in the street. I was so worried about dehumanizing myself by revealing that I couldn't connect to any young person. A void was filled with fear. When responsibilities grow, so do the reasons to go online. I'm always told that I should check this website, or book access online if I wanted to do anything. Time was running out for the spaces I had to just about get by. What prospects were there going to be? My housemate commented that whenever I got back from uni I would always look absolutely exhausted. I must have been working profusely to keep up with the obligations of a social world I'd felt cut off from. I seriously reflected that I was trying to catch up from being a waste of space after throwing a lot of time away. When my housemates had visits from old school friends, a sad wave submerged me into the deep again. Any friends from my time trying to be an online member was nowhere to be seen, in my own home city. I was less than the others because I didn't approach my old friends when they were only meters away from me at the bus stop.

If the troughs began to subside, it amazed me that such a casual interaction could miraculously swing my mood around. Bumping into a mate in the compost corner of computer clusters made it easy for my socials life to fester for the day.

"Fancy watching the game at the pub tonight?" If I could keep my public domain as a village-like environment, then I could sometimes crawl away from the post-traumatic paranoia. Emotions could get confused, but the best place to start was from the ground when things were difficult to get into focus.

There were times walking along the main road when I would bump into someone who'd invited me on a night out before I could say, "I need to get ready first." It was nice to not feel the need to switch attire or put make-up on. Plan or no plan, I got into the habit of always being prepared because the twisting and turning through a social life was the biproduct of people's relationship with the socials. Therefore, I adapted. If survival depended on company, then I made it easier to be drawn to me. To say that to anyone without carrying a phone would be madness, right? I eagerly found any reason to go to the supermarket in an area full of students to answer the conundrum. You adapt to survive.

My timetable was noted down on paper and kept in my rucksack. Half-way through my three-year course, I'd only checked my student email once, but I knew when and where I was scheduled to be. I tried to line it all up, although one morning I walked into a seminar to find the room completely empty. I had no one with me to say if it was cancelled or in a different room. There was already a lot of sweat rolling down my forehead from the cycle to campus, but I darted back towards an ATM to withdraw cash so I could claim a receipt that told me the time. I didn't want to turn up half-way through a class unaware of how late I was, so I regularly took a receipt from a transaction when alone and on the way somewhere. After zooming over to the library to log on to the student site, it said the class was running as usual on the contrary to what I'd just seen. It was now an hour after it was supposed to begin so I preferred to never find out. The whole scenario put me in a bit of a tailspin, and I wanted to avoid any familiar faces until the embarrassment left my immediate memory. I forget to wear a watch if I'm rushing. Unfortunately, the Smartphone had led to the decline of clocks in public places so the receipt trick (or asking a passing stranger who looked friendly enough) was the point of call. You adapt to survive.

4:6

"I saw you in a photo the other day!" someone at a bar greeted me. *How on earth?* She'd recognised me as her brother's friend, but we had never met before. At first, I believed that she must have got the wrong person, but then she introduced herself as the sister of one of my friends from school. She looked so different now – that was how much time had passed since my life in the online world. I knew that Facebook had a yearly reminder of posted pictures, so this must have been the explanation.

"How is he?" I asked, desiring to know despite the distance I'd caused.

She could see that I cared. "Message him! He told me the other day that he still sees everyone but doesn't see Luke anymore." We said goodbye and that was that. I turned back to my friend who sat opposite me and it was clear that I was dazed from the interaction.

"You should branch out," he sympathised. While I couldn't strategize how to do it without the socials, I felt the scenario stinging me like a bush of nettles, distracting my senses from the immediate surroundings as I failed to take my mind off the persistent flaring up of the pain. The socials were the wall between me and them, but there were little ways of making up for its functions in connectivity that I thought people would accept. Any options I could suggest for doing it differently were laughable. Ever since the start of uni, Grandma had been sending me newspaper cuttings about the football with a handwritten note. I wasn't at all embarrassed by it and my friends commented on how nice it was, but in practice, the smartphone reigned supreme with messaging. I felt ridiculous from some of the situations I got into without my phone on me. The day after the clocks went forward on the spring solstice, I turned up to work an hour late realizing in horror that business was well on its way in the garden centre. There was nothing waking me up with the adjusted time. As I rushed through to my department, colleagues were asking the obvious and laughing as I began my shift well after it should have started. At the very least I wasn't in trouble with my manager who saw the funny side. My guilt soon passed this time, although it did reveal how disjointed I'd become from the customs of other people. In another test of mental and physical fitness, I leapt into my faculty building to have my first one to one meeting with a tutor. I knocked on the door to their office breathing fast, and judged I was on time once I had observed his behaviour and unaccompanied status. Seeing personal bookshelves and no audience around me, he greeted me informally before asking about what I would like to specialise in.

"You can always email me if you've got any questions," all of them say at the end of a seminar. This was their profession and when it came to phrasing a title for a project for submission, students emailed them and got approval from their tutors within the space of one or two days and then began the writing about their research. Another purpose was to recommend texts to students depending on where their independent studies were going. Engaging in that way would maintain a sense of direction during the course knowing that more guidance could always be accessed online. With the way that I was outside normal procedure, I was constantly uncertain over how to research and where to look. Talking in the tutor's office was the way to stop myself from reading pages of stuff without knowing which bits were actually relevant. My project title was approved, but the long documentaries that could be found on YouTube were not ideal. The meeting was done and I didn't have to worry about contacting the tutor over the three-week break. But with another tutor it wasn't so straight-forward. The suggestion of emailing him made me compromise my idea as much as I could, seeing as I'd rather do an essay on something I wasn't too interested in over having to worry about any online consultation. People go about with convenience in mind, whereas for me, it was evasion. I was extremely lucky for an upcoming group presentation where I was grouped with the one person in the class whom I could arrange to see. She was a friend who'd lived in the halls with me, and we still frequently saw each other in our group gatherings. As the rest of our group exchanged profiles for making a chat, I felt secure that my friend was relatively aware of my social behaviour. But when I hadn't seen her for a couple of weeks, I began to worry. I knocked at her house to be told by her housemate that she was out. Incidentally, she happened to be my housemate's girlfriend, so I managed to indirectly arrange a meet-up. Individual parts were synced when a laptop was passed onto me. It almost disappointed me that other members of our presentation group didn't seem to care as much as I did while I was pulling my hair out and hoping that I could participate. By the end of it all, it had seemed so easy. Perhaps it was the process that initially made it big. I took part without being connected by everyone else's definition. That was a lot of work besides the task itself.

4:7

Uber was almost always the taxi of choice for all my friends who get around after dark. I only remember one occasion when I got a taxi with my friends from the local service, and that was because there was a rank at the bottom of the street where my mate sprained his ankle. Uber was an app, of course, and it was cheaper than the local cabs, so it was therefore winning my friends over without them giving it a second thought. When going into town with a bunch one evening, someone would summon a driver from their phone in a matter of minutes while tracking how close the vehicle was to announce when everyone should prepare to leave. If convenience was especially needed, the bus didn't match the standard Uber had set. Young people have a flexible social life conditioned from organizing everything with the socials. I even saw Uber's heading to uni from the city, and admittedly, I was in one of them heading there on a rainy day with my housemate. It was unknown to me how much money had been spent on Ubers that I've hopped in. Most of the time, my friends couldn't be bothered to chase the fraction of the cost that made up for my passage. It was quite inconvenient after such an easy ride, but I made sure to do nothing to bring down their Uber rating. Some drivers would refuse customers if the rating was below par, and people needed Uber to always be there for them. Convenience was their king.

The three-week break meant that all my housemates had left Brighton, so I had the house to myself. Saying goodbye to the last remaining friend I lived with, the atmosphere abruptly shifted from a hub of connection to a playground for all my intrusive thoughts. After less than two days, I moved back in with my family for the rest of the break. Campus was super quiet, and I was scraping motivation from the barrel. My village was gone, the network I learnt to cherish during its absence like the living thing it was. It was my saviour, but also my preoccupation when I knew everyone could chat whenever they wanted. My worries blurred my focus when I thought about how much could change in between contact. No network meant that I imagined myself being pushed out of a few social lives. It had all happened before.

"Luke, I need you to add me on Facebook so I can tag you in football videos." I was glad that I wasn't shown a screen this time but I read the casual line as dissatisfaction. On another occasion he put a hilarious sales pitch for Snapchat to me, showing that you can take videos of a rainbow-coloured waterfall streaming out of anyone's mouth who appears on camera shot. I took his phone from him to entertain him with the filter, swiping the screen and pulling a silly face much to his amusement. A supply of instant gratification had been delivered, although I didn't comment on whether I'd seriously download the app as I employed any guile to get past another difficult situation in front of my face. It's what the people want, isn't it? Respond to that normal moment by making rainbows stream out of your mouth. That's why the app keeps releasing funny filters to change the normality of the socials. It makes their users stick to them while they correspond with the mind's movements of the imagination. My defence mechanism was particularly put to the test when a game of dares was started after getting home from the pub with my housemates one night.

"Luke, I dare you to show us your phone!" I paused for a split second, and then stood up from the sofa, to go and dig up my device from the depths of my room. My smartphone was then thrusted in the air for all to see before the dare was then changed into letting my housemate take a selfie on it.

"You can't change the dare once it's already been done," I swiftly responded, turning back to return the device to the bottom of my suitcase in the cupboard. Opting out of the game, I said goodnight to the house and went to bed. The phone hadn't been switched on, but the scenario had contributed to a juicy bit of gossip that spread to people outside of the game.

"I heard that you got your phone out last night," my other housemate said, with his eyebrows raised. My uncomfortable life was gradually being uncovered, but the real question for them was why this was my way of life, although I certainly didn't describe it as such.

A family matter coming to my doorstep was enough to have me panic about revealing anything. It got nerve-wracking seeing a conversation between Mum and one of my new friends. You know, what would one tell the other and vice versa? I leapt into action with a huge squirm when I heard my housemate answer the door to her, asking Mum what she wanted to say while remaining queasy about the thinness of the wall between me and the five others in the front room. *Please make no mention of the phone. Please.* I dismissed my own mother as quickly as possible.

This awkward desperation played out differently when I got back from my parents' house after dark. Just as I'd been informed that people were coming for a gathering, I answered the door to an unexpected visitor who tried to follow everyone else indoors. It appeared to be Pesto! He wasn't allowed beyond the front door of my parents', but seemed to have snuck out and tailed me down the hill as I returned home. I shouted his name in alarm and thought about what to do. With no basket and no phone, it wasn't clear how I would get him back. I picked him up to be certain of his identity once I stopped fumbling around to get everyone out of the way and keep the cat calm. It had the same grey and black pattern as Pesto's fur but I remained unsure and rushed to a lamppost across the street, holding this unidentified cat high in the air so that the light could show into his dark green eyes and white chin fur. *Was it him? Wow, I'm going to have to say goodbye to the rest of the guests in my house to carry this one twenty minutes up the hill.* There was nothing else for it, but I triple checked by holding him high up beneath the light like he was Simba, realizing once I'd paused to think that this cat was heavy. Its tail was short too, while Pesto was quite slim and had a longer tail. False alarm! I must have looked like a maniac, but I had to be 100% sure. Moments later, my housemate approached me after coming back from the shop and I didn't know where to begin. I saw this lookalike a few days later, before dark, from the window of my front room. He seemed to enjoy entering people's homes, and this time leapt through an open window of the house opposite. After a few minutes, I saw two people at the window carefully placing the cat outside. I was playing a board game with my housemates and our neighbours noticed that we were watching the action pan out and an exchange of waves occurred with some sentences being written down big on paper. We ended up befriending this house and arranged to meet up a few times once they and my housemates had each other added on the socials. For once it was pen and paper that initiated things, while Pesto's lookalike added to the excitement of meeting fellow students. I was delighted to see one of their written signs hung up on the wall in their front room amongst a bunch of group photos.

4:8

The full-scale reality felt like incomprehensible nonsense when trying to imagine telling someone.

"You know you can tell me anything, Luke." A 'thank you' was all I could offer back. With time, however, friends became more accustomed to the fact that here I was, a friend of theirs without the electronic connection they deemed essential to life itself. But it was evidently challenging for them beyond the practical side.

"Where do you get your news from?" *People like you,* I almost said. I had to listen closely to the fragments of information coming from conversations to piece together a level of understanding of the world. It worked when I had my housemates, the people I owed my life to, but it didn't stretch as far as subjects that were of no interest to them. Nor events in my family for that matter. I knew Mum's cousin was seriously unwell, but I didn't find out that he passed away until I went to my parents a few days after.

"I tried to contact you but it went straight to voicemail again," Mum said. She and this relative were very close, while I was unavailable because of my own issues. I felt awful about it. Twenty-one years old, and I couldn't take responsibility. No excuses were made this time.

It's no wonder that a terrible feeling came from my gut when a mother gets her infant to approach me with a toy for sale at work: "Go on. Give it to the man so he can scan it." I wasn't a man. I was a failure who couldn't be there for my grieving family because of a behaviour over something I didn't even understand.

If I wasn't doing enough with my life, I would try to find a more natural way to cope when my peril with the no-phone problem made my relations with people feel unsteady. My housemate mused that he wouldn't know what to do if he had a new-born child and wanted me to celebrate the occasion with him. After seeing that this had grabbed the attention of the whole room, I then told him that he was one of the few people who could conjure up a dark magical spell that would make me appear before him. The comeback appeared to be socially acceptable to a question that had some deeply serious elements to it.

My ever-encroaching idea of an end of contact hit me especially hard at a farewell party for two of my friends doing a year abroad for the next stage. One of them was my housemate and there was truly a feeling for the event marking an end of an era. My alien status didn't obstruct the emotional connection that developed since the beginning of the halls. With nothing else for me to validate friendships when all the others had the socials, the thought of my housemate being in Canada, and another friend in the Netherlands, made me uncertain about my unsteady relationship with people and what they might become without any contact. I was so used to seeing these two almost every day. They didn't ask about what we'd do. More change. I was struggling to handle it while the nature of my lack of communication remained a secret. The friction of the contact issue burnt when remarks were given on the other side.

One familiar line was, "I would have invited you but I don't have a way of contacting you." The quantity of these complaints were hitting home and I was very insecure about what was built to last. It took a lot of work to scrape up an idea of success that corresponded with the reality of a position where I'll always be missing something. It continued its long, horrible trajectory that made me question if I was progressing in life at all? Dad rarely brought up the subject of my practical difference, but Mum couldn't hold off from feeding back to me that he said I needed to grow up. I couldn't tell if I was taking a step forward or a step back. Perhaps my isolated existence had gone nowhere, and I was simply fooling myself about getting away from the time when I was hidden away on my own. It was hard to know anything.

4:9

When deciding what to do for housing for the next academic year, my housemates and I thankfully had our interests aligned by agreeing to renew our tenancy. No one fancied moving their stuff. If convenience was king by online rule, then convenience was king offline too. From my point of view, staying in the same place meant I didn't have to do as much online, so I went along with it. On the other hand, one of our members was leaving to Canada, so we had to replace them with a single housemate who hadn't already sorted something out. The latter ruled out all our friends at uni who weren't seeking an arrangement solo, so we were left to find someone completely new. The most established way of doing this was on a Facebook page. Local students popped up after my housemate made a post. An individual was selected and I was shown their profile picture for approval before he was invited over to meet everyone. That was it: an online conversation and a swift judgement of a profile, then the next stage proceeded. It was surreal meeting our choice in person as I was far from accustomed to doing meet-ups from an online base. Clap the dust off our hands. Our work was done and he was moving in at the end of the summer. I was thinking about what he would make of my phoneless situation. He was totally new and we were going to be living together for a year in a house of four. It wasn't someone from the halls who had shared their experience of uni with me. This was a new mind, and his life was going to take a weird turn because of me alone.

I wasn't looking forward to the summer. No one was going to be home for the best part of it while they spent time in their hometowns seeing the people outside of their uni lives. There were meet-ups being planned and interwoven in between, although it took some measures to help people understand how they would initiate.

"How will you know?" my friend asked after we discussed a summer plan.

"I'm here right now in front of you. What's the plan?" Nope. That didn't work. All quiet.

Back at my parents, my head had gone back in time to exactly the year before when I took up to six days a week again in the same retail routine that proved to be soul destroying to the non-gardener. I didn't have a true right to complain, but I got fed up. My mood had submerged much further below the Earth's crust, to intensify the fire in my head. The support network of my friends was suspended. At least being at my parents meant I was spared the questioning for a time. It was refreshing to go back without having to prepare to deflect anything like usual.

4:10

I'd left my days free in advance for a specific weekend. Waiting for my housemate and his girlfriend to arrive back at the house after seeing none of my mates for over a month, it turned out the reason for their return had in fact been cancelled, but they wanted to come down anyway. It was a no-phone classic. During a board game later that day, a photo was sent to a couple of the others that made them ask about me. It was a world apart from my isolation a few hours beforehand and a firm reminder of the positive force that my friends had restored into my life. Without these heroes, I was empty and bleak like an abandoned house in the middle of nowhere. Instead, the outcome of their role determined that I could identify as a person again.

It's no myth that feeling better about yourself is never a linear curve. In a matter of days before my friends killed the pain for an evening they'd spent with me, I recognised him instantly, just like all the other times I've seen him around the small city of Brighton. He came into the garden centre and we looked at each other from about ten meters. Without the double look, I walked on as he strolled around on the phone to someone. He was what people would call a lifelong friend, having met me when we were both at the age of four in the first days of school. We hadn't connected since I was eighteen during the dying days of my online life. He was always kind and generous to me whether I was at my highs or lows. Going to different secondary schools is always a massive test, but we stayed in touch throughout intervals lasting as long as a whole year. Time didn't matter because of the friendship it was.

Now it was over three years but I shouldn't have cared. We passed again a few minutes after the eye contact, and the opportunity was there.

"Alright?" I greeted, but not in the friendly manner I'd had on all those other times to him throughout my life.

"Hey." He looked like he was ready to stop and chat, but I was petrified. We'd known each other so well. We didn't need any online validation to affirm the bond between us, unlike so many others whom I used to know. But I wasn't ready. I panicked and walked on. Five minutes later, I swore under my breath and felt terrible. My old friend was always less imposing and shyer than the people I went to school with. Why couldn't I have had it in me to simply utter words towards him and hear whatever it was he had to say. I'd barred myself from doing the right thing for someone who had done so much for me for fourteen years, and I'd blocked his companionship from my system even though he had nothing to do with my issue. *Go back and find him!* There he was, looking at something for sale. I wanted to approach him, but this failed to overpower the cognitive programming that told me to flee from any old face who was around during the time when I was online. Going back to try a third time, I held my breath and walked in his direction. I was ready to engage now, fighting everything that was pulling me back from a person who cared about me. Our mums had seen each other in the street a year before and told one another what was happening in our lives. I'd heard about a rough experience he had been going through. *Let's rekindle the friendship so we can support each other once again like those hundreds of times before. Go!* I stopped walking and pretended to be busy working. There was now someone with him whom I didn't recognise. Every morsel of determination I pathetically tried to prepare was flattened in an instant. I didn't engage. I stayed well out of the way of them. They left and carried on with their day. I was full of a density of lament that span my head around like a power drill. It was all on me. I was a failure, and this was another piece of evidence to prove it. *What was I? Not who.* Overthinking everything was an understatement. I couldn't wait to see my uni friends again so that I could have a backbone inside of me.

Walking back from work one evening, I headed down to check on my student house. As I came closer, I failed to realise right away that my housemate was calling my name from the window of a car that slowed down next to the curb on the pavement. I was back again in the place and a switch flicked. Apparently, they'd driven a route they speculated I'd walk from work after missing me there by a fraction. Their success came from intuition. The idea of doing that in advance would probably have made them anxious seeing as they don't usually plan to handle things like that. It's laudable for it, and spontaneity can be a stimulant for excitement. I found it puzzling when my housemate asked if I'd sent our friend a text message wishing him a happy birthday.

"It must have been a prank," I figured, "I don't even have his number." It was life-affirming to have other people having a bit of fun with the dynamic. We deduced that the culprit was a close friend who had already joked about making me a Facebook account to see how people would react. The light-hearted irony was very welcome. It was harmonizing me and this circle so that it softened the emotional swingathon when I saw some old faces at a Brighton-based festival doing their thing. I quietly watched on deep in thought while my large-framed sunglasses and longer hair acted as a decent enough disguise. Old members wouldn't undermine my resurrection anymore. There was nothing left to lose from back then.

4:11

Time was really running out and my back was against the wall.

"Did you bring your phone, Luke?" Mum asked, while we were on holiday.

My prevacation persisted, "Yeah."

"Where is it?"

"In my bag, back at the hotel."

"Why is it there and not on you?"

"I forgot it."

"You didn't bring it away with you at all did you?" The tone of the conversation went from an interrogation to a big telling off.

"That was the last gift Grandma and Grandpa got you before Grandpa died, and you don't even use it!"

At this point, I forgot we were out in public and I completely flipped, "Why do you have to say it like that?! Why do you have to bring Grandpa into this?" There was nothing but red heat in my body, venting out into blasts until it eventually extinguished into sulky silence. We were on the Greek island of Mykonos, and I could tell where the spots were for pretty photos trending on Instagram when I observed what people were doing. Sat at a restaurant opposite one spot where turns were taken for the shot, I was inquisitive rather than disgruntled. The scene didn't really bother me in the slightest. I said no without a thought when my friend asked if it bothered me when everyone in the room was on their phone. If anything, that was my way of using it safely. It's what people do, and without being haunted by my experience with the socials, I wanted to be with people. When my friends were using them, it could still feel like a lifeline, since a lot of their lives were put into motion by them on a singular track where each respective member was crossing paths. It was the closest thing to an immediate solution. I knew that relying on people with this was unsustainable, but it kept me going, and I knew that things were going to change. I just didn't know how. As for my family, something else had to happen.

"The last time you sent me a text message was August 2016. That was three years ago," Mum complained. My parents remained unconvinced that I tried to text them in Italy before receiving their emergency messages. My defence went down the angle of contradicting that, but then I was ordered to show my phone. There was no way out.

"Is it on?" Mum asked.

"Out of battery." I didn't know this but that was the reply that came.

"Where's the charger?" I'd intentionally left it upstairs, and dragged my feet behind me as I went to fetch it. Mum made a guess that my phone was damaged in some way but as far as I was aware, it was perfectly fine. I put the phone on charge, leaving it face down on the carpet before leaving the room for a few minutes. My hands were trembling. There are so many different names for phobias. If there wasn't one for this then I would have exemplified it. I grabbed the phone after a few minutes, when I knew it would automatically turn on, swiftly unlocking it with my thumbprint and ignoring the following buzzes as I went straight to the contact list. There was a glimpse of names I'd forgotten were even there before I rushed past them to send Mum a full stop. Once I checked that it had gone through, I turned it off and threw it into a drawer.

"There you go!" I announced. "I've sent you a text and it's working."

"So you're going to use it, yes?" Mum asked.

"Yes, I'm using it!" I was panting from the episode. How could it be that bad? I was years apart from when the problem developed, but now I'd felt it reawaken and put me in distress as there were memories flashing across the front of my mind. It wasn't a world I wanted to go back to, and using my phone for the most basic purpose put me there. I curled up in bed and massaged my temples. How much time did I have left? I was soon starting the final year of my degree. After that, there were no plans. I was barely coping already, as it felt like my responsibilities were growing, and life's inevitable movements were going to cost me a future. Grandma, intending to go to a small house her and Grandpa had owned on the north coast of France, needed another family member to go with her for the journey on the train and the ferry. I'd spent many times there as a child, but back then, Grandpa was around to drive everyone. Now my family were entrusting me with the care of Grandma while she had the smartphone, and therefore the means of updating the rest of the family. For a quivering mess who couldn't even carry a mobile, I had a big task, but it would be one of the last times Grandma would go to this very sentimental place that she and Grandpa had built up for decades. I had to go ahead with it all. Whether that was sensible of me was another question. I had no real indication as to whether I was mentally fit enough to embark on this. I supposed one good thing was that at least the house had no Wi-Fi.

4:12

The unimaginable was happening, just as Grandma and I were approaching the shores on the ferry back from France. A smartphone was in Grandma's hands, taking a selfie of us both to send to the family group chat on WhatsApp. I had to laugh. She'd only been using a smartphone for a year, and it was the only one between the two of us to notify everyone about our progress. Each reply was read out afterwards. Grandma asked if I had the Instant Messenger, a total distortion of the generational divide in people's relationship with the online realm. I had gone cold turkey when I was eighteen, and my grandmother was getting me involved with a key feature.

Arriving back in Brighton from a week away, I was experiencing a strange sensation that I could only describe as a set of hallucinations. My walk through the town centre left me fixating on people's faces in my peripheral vision because they appeared to be the faces of different individuals whom I've known throughout my life. I turned my head this way and that to put them in the front of my vision, only to find that they were only strangers who happened to look like familiar people. It put me on edge. I wasn't sure if the sweat on my forehead was from carrying a large bag in the heat or from my nerve-injected uncertainties. My pace picked up to get home sooner. The first person I saw there was my housemate, who added a different spin by growing a massive beard during a summer road trip that made him hard to recognise. I was so thrown off by everything that I wasn't assertive enough to tell him that I'd go straight to my room after he requested me to hold back from entering while discussing something with his girlfriend. When I moved on to reach my parent's house, I was finally able to find a mildly comfortable headspace.

My third year at uni was commencing, and friends were showing their faces less. There was more time spent studying so the gatherings grew noticeably smaller. My new housemate was coming in barely knowing any of my friends outside the house so my point of contact with people had dispersed. It was less of an everyday village so my connections felt dimmer.

My now cleanshaven housemate was saying that if my way with technology stayed the same, then one day I'd be "Fucked." I had to hold off the temptation to retort that I was already indeed faring that way. I noticed immediately that my learning environment had changed when I sat in my first seminar for the academic year. Out of the thirty students in the room, there was only one notepad and pen being used, and it was mine. Everyone else had a laptop, the volume of the typing giving me a clue as to how interesting a point was for the class. The lecture hall had nearly as many laptops as students. One time, there were plenty more notepads in class when I was there, but now that things were stepping up a gear with the mention of the dissertation, investments were made, and the laptop became everyone's notepad. A lot of my paper was scrounged from the leftovers of my grandparents' teaching careers. I wondered which was quicker out of the pen and the laptop for noting key points, and which was better overall for learning, not discounting the potential for distraction. My housemate, who studied history like me, didn't comment on the efficiency of writing digitally, although apparently *Football Manager* ran very well on his new laptop.

For my main study module for the year, I had a tutor who confessed that technology wasn't his friend when it came to teaching. He had deliberately chosen a classroom with a whiteboard, and picked up his marker pens to clarify what we were focusing on from the readings. Here, I was more engaged, and I knew I'd picked the right option when the content also grabbed me. The only problem was that I had to think about how to do a solo presentation, when all the other students were plugging in their laptops to get up a slide show on a projector. I instinctively picked a topic for later in the term. At least I didn't have to worry about communicating with a group for it. The tutor was giving us handouts for the topics so I figured I could emulate it. There was only a small number in the class and I happened to have credit for the printers on campus. Evasive manoeuvres once again. The more informal atmosphere of the smaller class was a great opportunity to improve on public speaking – a good skill if I wasn't going to be using the internet to express myself to people.

4:13

I figured a society at uni would be good to try for the first time when there were less people around. They were all organised online but my housemate was eager to try out ultimate frisbee and our close friend was captain for the university team. I turned up to a trial not too fussed, but it was a way to get out and socialise through sport. My fitness was good, but I had nothing else that this team could make good use for so I didn't stretch beyond the free taster. Happily, my housemate signed up so it was worthwhile considering he needed it on his schedule to help get through a recent breakup. I'd lived with this friend for over two years by this point. It was my turn to be there in a life crisis. I couldn't organise a social gathering within my means but I could try to always be sociable in the house for him. My newest housemate and I were also becoming fast friends, but like always, I didn't talk about the phone until he found out for himself.

"Do you not even carry a phone?" he asked cautiously, knowing that he was touching on a personal matter. I murmured an answer to this very direct question. It amazed me that meeting anyone and having a joint interest could inspire them to state, "I'll message you," just as you're about to say, "Nice to meet you, I'll see you around." This exact conversation occurred after playing football with a group and then being asked if I wanted to join a local team. Deep down, I was up for it, although I didn't end up seeing him around, so I never chased it up. I failed to branch out in my own way, so I opted to do more with the people from the halls where it all started. The village held up despite the quiet. Before I knew it, my two friends spending a year abroad came back to visit on separate occasions. It might not be every day, by my insecurity held off on the occasion when we picked things up where we left off. One of them had even kept his scheduled return a secret from all but one of our friends, and surprised the rest. It was a perfect boost for me as he jumped out at me in my own house when I got back from a shoddy day. Despite the socials, the plan wasn't leaked by anyone, so I would have been in the same position as my friends. When a lot of changes are happening, and someone shows you that some things remain the same, the meaning of relationships in your life becomes a lot clearer. It was often refreshing to feel it without the conspicuous associations on the socials that used to be the lens conditioned in me from my teens. It's no wonder my sense of security clung to a relationship when my housemate showed a photo of us both at the masquerade ball that he'd posted on his Instagram. We'd already lived together for a while yet the symbolic nature of that post completely changed how I felt. Pride and validity can be highly sensitive to anything on the socials. It enlarges the online world within the mind so more reasons to go there rise at an exponential rate. The implications of a gesture between people who know each other, even distantly, keeps them checking. I could never have anticipated how much I was thinking about this trend after dropping it all. How much had my mental life really been affected by it? It was incalculable, while my thoughts drifted to all the people around me using it when I no longer did. That was fact, but I didn't seem to fix any conclusion of my issue as to being either a small thing, therefore rendering me pathetic and inferior, or being massive on a scale that made me messed up on an emergency level. Both emotional proportions could be unkind. Whatever I was thinking, it was unstable, and my attitude rapidly changed from needing company to locking myself away from it again. My newest housemate became disheartened by the latter.

"Don't go to bed. It's nine o'clock!" he moaned. People were curious about what I was doing in my room if I didn't have anything connected to the Wi-Fi. No games console, no computer – there was nothing to do in there. I knew that, but that was the point. I wanted to vanish for the rest of a long day, because my life was exhausting. A more comprehensive reply was that I was reading, but I also worried my friends would start to think that I was boring. Video games were given a try when I was in the right frame of mind, but the VR headset would have been a step too far. The rest of the house can keep the controller when that one is out. Evolution didn't make these things more accessible to me. It just made it a bit scarier for my PTSD.

4:14

I didn't want to turn this down only because I couldn't be contacted. It hadn't happened yet, despite me saying 'yes' several times already. At this point, my housemate conceded that he wasn't going to make me use a phone by the end of uni. He had grown used to the missing link in a way that I couldn't have anticipated when we first became friends. He was one of my heroes who made my uni experience what it was. If the fond times he'd contributed to didn't happen, I thought that I was going to die. Now he went even further by taking the postal address of my family home to write to me over the winter break. He could see that I genuinely wanted to visit him in London, and the weight of a group meet-up made it extra significant. The letter was later than expected and he apologised, saying that it took some time to reach a final settlement with the group and purchase the tickets. With the gap between postage and delivery, he'd bought my e-ticket knowing that the price was going to rise when it was closer to the event. It was all looking feasible, until I realised that I wasn't going be able to write back in time. Before I could invent any doubts, I grabbed my parent's landline phone, dialled his number that was left in the letter and heard his voice on the other end of the phone for the first time. Surprised, but comfortable, he listened to me while I was nervous about how he'd tell our friends about this momentous phone call. I prayed that the landline still had free calls in the evening like once before. He mentioned that our friend was also making the journey from Brighton, the same one I'd got a high grade in the group presentation we did with the aid of her compassion. Complications aside, I made it to the first meet-up outside the city of my uni. If it wasn't for my companion on the train, I would have had to arrange a time and a place at Victoria station. As if it wasn't challenging enough for everyone already.

My host was wary. We were in an enormous venue, put together out of separate ones, for an event holding thousands. I couldn't wander off. My time with my friends would be over if I managed to lose them.

But after I and one other went searching for a missing member, my housemate yelled, "Don't leave me again!" I was supposed to be staying at his place, so he was right to express his worry about losing me for the rest of the night. I realised that I was distracting him from letting his hair down if he was babysitting me on a London night out. He also called an Uber to get us home for the evening when the underground was shut. The convenience king had lent its services again, summoned from the smartphone to make everyone feel secure.

It was drilled into me that the necessity of a mobile was to be avoided. I couldn't decide on anything but to play a waiting game while I was afraid of going haywire by reactivating it. One evening, I held my smartphone in my hands, turning it, caressing it, brushing my thumb over the on button. *Shall I just do it?* There were people I wanted to contact, although I didn't have their numbers. Switching it on could lead to me to go on Facebook and search their name, perhaps astounding someone by accepting a friend request so I could filter a search on a list of mutual friends. You usually go further to find what you seek, and you'll be given more than you wish for in the process. No. I stopped myself from applying pressure on the button. It didn't feel right. The phone went back in the suitcase.

My landline calls cost money. My smartphone had free unlimited calls. One of the first conversations I had with Mum in the new year was about her phone bill. More questions incoming; more lies. I grew paranoid about being in some real trouble. If I didn't use my phone like everyone in my life was wishing me to do, I could sometimes feel like my whole existence is fundamentally wrong. I wasn't taking responsibility, so I grew afraid that I could get fired from my job or kicked out of uni at any moment. Was I less of a friend by being so stressed about all this making me less fun or supportive? People were worrying about points of contact. My housemate asked me what would happen if I got hit by a car.

BAM! It took place when I was cycling home from uni during rush hour. A black hatchback swerved out at a junction and I flew onto their bonnet and down to the ground. Before I could look up, the driver sped away from the incident and members of the public were rushing in to help. I was then sat on a chair, unhurt but accompanied by someone who was talking me through the shock. They soon asked if I could phone anyone once they saw that I was unscathed. I was only a hundred meters from my house but someone stayed with me for a while before I went on. Again, my dependency beckoned anyone around me to give more of their time and effort. This kind lady was late for work by stopping in her tracks for me. How much time would it take until no one could help me if my real problem remained a secret?

4:15

It was time to step up to the plate and talk. I had been allotted the topic for the presentation on my own and I'd printed several copies of a handout. There was no slide show and no devices to engage the class with. I didn't think until it got closer to the time about the more awkward choice of discussing visual arts, so I had to pay extra for printing images in colour. Monochrome wasn't going to do any justice to Henri Matisse's brightly coloured paintings. I almost couldn't believe that everyone appreciated the presentation style, my relatively technophobic tutor included. I did it differently, and it worked! It wasn't impossible without using the laptop to learn, or helping others learn. I'd felt myself reaching a successful goal because of the challenge for me to present projects to people. It was timely, considering I was preparing myself for the possibility of dropping out. Despite my secret, something changed in me. It had all worked out without me scraping through it. I put my own seal on something that was met with appraisal from a university professor. I wasn't avoiding the moment. Instead, I made it. It was the first-time public speaking had a confident flavour from my relationship with the online world, a relationship that before would always dampen what I felt I could do in front of anyone. I even lost track of time doing it. An hour was up when my presentation finished. I didn't hide, I came out to animate what I was interested in and bridge my damaged mind to a healthy directive. I brought myself closer to real people again.

All the speakers were connected via Bluetooth, and everything would be streamed online. I was so used to seeing it reach the senses of the people in the room while my control over the source was rarely of my own accord. Since my consumption of music depended on whom I was with, getting a record player for Christmas from Dad was magical besides the passion itself. I wasn't a technophobe, I was consuming music, but offline. Not to mention my friends appreciated it too. People liked records in the online organised world because the formats still got something special to give. High street entertainment stores were saved by the taste for them when CD's, DVDs, and many other areas of offline shopping had been usurped by the virtual points of consumption. I was intensely grateful to just feel okay from using something that aligned with my digital evasion. It was also quite nice to say no to someone asking if my speakers could be plugged into an AUX cable. *Your powers won't work here.* But I would have been naïve if I'd thought that my deep-seated issue could be overcome by the evasive habits I used to swerve around a whole multiverse worth of outreach. How much longer was I going to last from living like this? Where was I going to go if I couldn't face the music in full? Waiting for an idea of wellness solidifying in me didn't seem to be working, but it was the only measure I knew how to take. Something would have to happen externally for me to change how I was behaving.

Going to my parents' house one afternoon, it must have been about the hundredth time Mum tried to get to the bottom of it all. I sat in silence for a few seconds thinking for a little without putting up a defence. Time slowed right down. Why wasn't I using it? That's all it was in practice really. I'd signed out, logged off, put it on standby, and hidden everything away. If there was something else in the equation, I could never truly depict it all for someone's mind to fathom. I hadn't lost the phone or broken it. Perhaps I thought that technology was evil and I needed to go to a psychiatric ward to live out this woeful life I'd entered. I was scared to answer in case it would lead to that outcome. I had disintegrated and my own word was about to prove it. But then I had been going on for so long, doing things and trying to help people. My friends had proven to me that it can be comfortable talking about things that would otherwise be kept close to their chests in case they aren't accepted as real people. We can feel bad for filling the ears of others with our problems, or think that someone might look at us differently afterwards. We could hold back with that thought in mind, or talk so that support can be received. I looked up from the floor, preparing to use words to articulate something that no one had ever heard.

"I can't," I said. "I can't use any of it." I'd already closed the door to the front room so that my sister didn't hear me telling Mum about the problem that became the only life I'd known. Tears began to obscure my eyes. My body seemed to have lost all feeling as I poured out my version of mental illness towards Mum who was sitting still listening intently. I couldn't take going all the way and letting her soak in the possibility that I wouldn't have lived long enough to tell the tale of my monstrosity.

"This isn't surprising to me, Luke," she said first, "We're going to get you some help."

Finally, I talked. Relief would come now that the process could be put into the helping hands of other people after the fall.

Part V

5:1

Something was telling me that I wasn't experiencing the worst outcome. It was always there throughout it all, even when I didn't have any idea what it was. My memory had nothing missing, flicking back at all the fleeting instances that add up to an overall feeling. Whatever space my head was in, black hole, galaxies far away, asteroid fields, or a calm place on planet Earth, a conscious idea travelled through it all, even when I disliked it during the difficult times. I was very alert that it was there for the next few days after telling Mum about my problem. After being made a cup of tea and some food, I sat in silence reflecting on the bridge that had just been created between myself and the rest of the world. Friends had given me enjoyment at uni. Substantial things had happened that affirm life itself. Yes, I couldn't satisfy the need for social interaction via the socials, but it meant that for every moment I felt alone after dropping off the virtual habitat, it increased the value I placed in human interaction altogether. I was deluded if I thought that I was imprisoned. My isolation couldn't misinform me that I shouldn't speak about it forever. The rubbish doesn't vanish by leaving it in the bin, whilst it'll end up preventing future space for further waste. Mum told me that I was too young to deal with my problem effectively on my own. I hadn't learnt how to, and my self-teaching made me more anxious about it over time. She knew that I always loved going to cafés ever since she was pushing me in a buggy, so we would go to one where I could be comfortable appreciating the changes in life since I entered one last. Café culture and walks around the green spaces of the city always kept me calm. That was the start of seeking help. Talking, moving, and organizing would be made easier from here. I didn't bother telling the rest of my family, but I sensed that they knew. With extra briskness, my cousin was being told to put her tablet away during a family get together.

I felt a resolve in my steps. Riding on the back of the non-digitised presentation I did, I went to my tutor's office to talk about the final project for my degree. I was taken aback a little when he'd lent me a couple of his own books to study instead of telling me where to access materials online. One of them was more related to my other module he wasn't teaching me which was thoughtful in benefitting a working relationship that enriched my education. So much so that I told him I was thinking of taking it further by applying to do a master's degree. The hurdles of working remotely didn't deter me from my interest in history. Books will always be cool within the craft – I knew that by stepping into a tutor's office. But unfortunately, my favourite out of the options for postgraduate courses weren't supervised by this individual tutor. A debate filled my head whether I should sacrifice my preferences to resume the safety of being taught by his offline style. I decided the application had to wait. It was a tricky decision when considering the opportunities stretching to offline contact. It was that which kept me in the race without the wheels falling off. And then before I could think more about it, a four-week wave of strikes was happening at the university while I had no idea what my final projects were going to be about. Without any guidance, my motivation suffered. Getting out of bed in the cold mornings of winter became one of the toughest parts of the day. I had to do something to shrug off the circumstantial emptiness. That's when I popped my head into the camera of my housemate's phone video calling our friend in Canada.

"How would you like it if I came to visit?" I beamed. I correctly predicted that I wouldn't be the only one wanting to go in the terms break, so same as Ukraine, the flights were booked for me and I paid back the debt. It was good to have an errand during the strikes of heading to the bank to sort it, despite the anxiety around staff interactions taking hold, with the knowledge that not many young adults stay off online banking. The staff would always ask. They knew customers wanted convenience as king. I powered through my peculiar barrier to have a trip to look forward to. It didn't matter that the online world wasn't filling my time in a period that invited ennui back in the house because I was soon going to visit my close friend in Toronto.

5:2

The downers of disruption can be dealt with when you make plans, but talk of the people around me made me hear about the distant panic of the spread of a viral infectious disease. The affair in Asia was brought to my mind when it reached headline news, but the science behind the contagion was unclear as reports about the issue spreading to northern Italy were being pushed into immediate attention. By the time I entered my front room to hear my housemate saying that there were apparent cases in London, there was an atmosphere that made me think of a leadup to nuclear fallout. Everyone was under the impression that it was nearing the end of everything and the World Health Organization was the final thing being quoted before it was announced that Britain was going into full lockdown. People's worlds were going to become dramatically smaller, while every saving grace I thought I had was taken away from me. My visit to Canada and in-person teaching had collapsed. Mental health was being predicted to be more vulnerable and all my support was put on hold whilst I tried to cope between now and then without knowing how long we'd be staying in our homes for. When the prime minister's broadcast was played on TV, I was saying out loud that I was done for.

"We all are…" my housemate replied. Lockdown of course, was a collective experience, so anything I expressed regarding my illness wouldn't come across as important. I went upstairs to wallow alone.

My days were restricted to outdoor solo exercise, supermarket queues, and whatever people did in the household. Social distancing was enforced by law. I preferred to stay at mine with a couple of my housemates. My parents had been told a few days before and they understood that I didn't want to be entirely cut off from my friends while I remained offline. There was no alternative to interact with anyone else. My feed was the voice of those in the room and only them. Mum told me that I could knock on the front door and talk from a distance, considering it could be argued that my medical condition warranted it. She was insistent that the crisis didn't change that I needed access to professional help, regardless of not relating it to a type of diagnosis. Other platforms for contact would be bolstered while it was believed to be unsafe for anyone to engage outside the household. My need for in-person companionship had never felt so alien when everyone was filling their time with services I couldn't consume, but this didn't stop me from trying out something new. I decided that it was time to pick up a musical instrument, a hobby I'd never pictured myself doing until it presented itself in front of me with its appeal. My house had borrowed a couple of guitars from friends not long before they evacuated to their folks'. Both my housemates were also keen, so it became an activity for us to bond over as we shared different tunes that we thought would be fun to play during the empty months. With them getting as into it as me, the inconvenience of being tone-deaf could be resolved by an app on their smartphones to tune the instruments if need be. I noted down sections of songs to learn from searching them on my housemate's PlayStation. While they ate the hours with their games, I could hold my favourite guitar and enjoy an activity that kept my mind off my woes. The first two weeks of lockdown were the worst as I felt my life shrink and slow way down. After that, however, I stopped worrying about the future, because with the whole globe in crisis, the pressures I'd felt before had gone. It was okay to underachieve. That was what was going to happen from all the disruption anyway. The aim of compensating for my incompleteness after losing touch was no longer a pressing matter that put me in distress. My social life was overshadowed by the people my age whom I saw over my shoulder, but it became clear that they were experiencing this affair like I was, and the virtual space could never equate to the successes people would reach if the restrictions weren't in place. I wasn't being left behind here. My frustration dimmed every time I woke up in the morning as there was little to keep up with. People were merely instructed to hang in there.

What was hard for me to see was how the socials were changing as people's usage of them was changing. TikTok was an example of another step in their development. I'd heard it had been recently released in Britain a short while before lockdown and its popularity exploded during the abundance of spare time. One of the first things my housemate did when he woke up was to play short videos featuring trending jingles or songs. I assumed wrongly at first that this was Instagram, but no. This was a newer titan that influenced the user's interests in a much faster, effective way, with its algorithms making it smarter than a lot of the socials put together. Entertainment and information to the user's liking were tweaked by this super engine to architect what they wanted to see on their screens just by reading the response to different content. As an activity, it could erase anyone's memory of having a mini library in arms reach from the toilet. The sounds of TikTok became a staple for locked doors to the bathroom. It's given influence a new meaning as anything catching the eye could effortlessly bring unlimited stocks of videos straight back to the user. A choice of data on the socials could transform your stream of consciousness wherever you are. Lockdown had also brought live streams of music from a studio. Sets were designed for a venue but performed through the virtual medium. So, there was a lot to do, while I had all the time in the world to observe my thoughts.

5:3

The decline of public activity didn't change that my parents were adamant about me talking to a counsellor. After Mum got through to someone on the phone, she told me that she gave a brief description of my problem. I couldn't yet receive any face-to-face treatment, but I could book an appointment over the phone. I sensed a lot of people with ongoing mental health issues would prefer face-to-face, but I was trying to work out in the street outside my parents' house if there was any point in talking to a professional on a call. Weighing costs and benefits didn't really add up to anything so I made an instinctive decision on the spot. I was going to speak to a counsellor about my phone problem, through the phone.

On the other end of the line, a general NHS mental health support worker introduced herself, and asked me to give an account of my illness and the practical consequences that resulted from it. I had to go into my parents' garden with everyone in the house out of the way, answering the call at a specific time on Mum's smartphone. Being too public, I couldn't do it in the street or break the normal precautions of being in a different household. A multiple-choice questionnaire was put to me and then I was informed about what service was suitable for my condition. With comparisons of the socials with drugs being common knowledge, the professional recommended contacting a local support organization that usually dealt with alcohol and drug addiction. But an in-person service was suspended for the foreseeable, and as much as I didn't feel too bad from the call, she could tell that doing more sessions over the phone wasn't worth pursuing further. I got off the phone reassured at first, but I was on hold from anything substantial. The wait would last until lockdown was over, whenever that would be. I had written down some features of the session for now, and found that I'd strongly agreed that I'd let my family down, but I'd also strongly agreed that I was able to enjoy doing things. Nothing was clear cut at all here. Since time had stopped indefinitely, I had to wait for whatever the world was going to be when people could come together offline again.

Meanwhile, my housemates were talking about a group call with friends for a pub-style quiz every Friday evening. It became the highlight of their week, so they tried to persuade me to get involved, or else I'd apparently miss out. A brief individual call was manageable for me, but I didn't think I could take a group session for a whole evening, opting to go to my room to avoid being reeled in. Relationships with online life had turned on their head. Mine remained minimal, as grievous as that was during the highlight social gathering. I gave no reason for my absence, and I was still so mysterious to everyone that someone made a quiz which included three questions about me for several people to boggle their brains with.

"Which model of phone does Luke own?" was a test for the participants. Gladly, I had a reason to be on someone's mind then.

I often eavesdropped on my next-door neighbours, a bunch of students who regularly sat and talked in their garden. Given that my feed of what my age-group was thinking was limited to the people in my household, my curiosity kept my window open for a long time to hear political debates and music reviews fall into my use of the socials second-hand. I was finding whatever way to keep myself updated.

"It's okay, Luke. We can be like your secretary," Mum said from the doorway. I had given her access to my email and drafted something for her to send to my tutor without revealing the complication about our point of contact. A few days later, the response to it was addressed to me as I didn't follow Mum's wishes to let the university know about my circumstances.

"Luke! Great to hear from you. Hope you've been well," my tutor began. The intro suggested that he had been waiting for an update with my studies. It had been a long while, and having received no guidance, my initial idea was shut down immediately. My spirits sagged. Ignorance is bliss. There was a lot he sent to me, so my parents printed his emails seeing as it was going to take several readings for me to grasp it. I needed all the help I could get, but the method of learning was shaky. I wasn't sure how much more reading I should be doing so my whole project had its structure put on standby. I could only hope that these unprecedented conditions for finishing a degree could adjust how nice the marking process would be. It turned out that I couldn't get a result any lower than what my total marks had added up to in total throughout uni. The knowledge of a pass being all that was necessary confirmed the abandonment, with only half the class attending an online seminar that my housemate joined through his laptop. Oddly comforting. The collective experience gave reasons for everyone to receive a bit of extra help. My individual needs were less alien – I simply got the heading when my housemates checked their student accounts. It was like getting a mouthful of oxygen after thinking I was about to drown, the light dipping in and out of the water to shine towards the way out.

My parents gave me their dinosaur laptop to type up my projects. With work submitted online, my notepad and pen were almost made redundant. Social distancing killed it off, although my notes were still on paper. I was last to be added to the list of bedroom workers, even shifting back my sleep pattern in accordance with my housemates so I could see them in their waking hours. The garden centre was closed for business so it looked like I eventually needed to redeploy video games for entertainment, offline that is.

In the corner of my eye, I saw my housemate looking at me enquiringly before he commented, "I've never seen you play games like this before." It was an extraordinary time, but pigs don't fly. My attention moved on to giving arts and crafts a go. We had a mountain of uncollected recycling that put together whatever creative clogs I had to distribute it all somewhere. The result was a gigantic stegosaurus.

"What is that!?" my housemate cried when he came down from a gaming session. He had online multiplayer games; this was my pastime. If it was ever interpreted as exotic, then my things to do in lockdown brought back the joke that I should have an Instagram account made for me. My housemates went as far as the creation process, but I think they either needed my email address, or for one of them to have theirs free from their own profiles. I was indifferent, but it was funny to hear that my newest housemate had only just discovered my antique account on Facebook.

"I can't find it! I really want to find it. Where is it?" he said across from me. "Ah, there you are." He began examining the numbers of likes and comments on a couple of my photos, asking who my former acquaintances were.

I was pondering about whether I would need treatment by the time that social distancing wouldn't cover medical appointments.

There was no date set for the break from the monotonous ghost town. My mental compass had altered, that was for sure. I even began to show a newfound willingness to talk to my parents' neighbours across the street now that everyone had no exclusive commitments elsewhere. I'd derailed from my digital divide aware that people had their moving lives, whereas the stillness in lockdown was a great opportunity for me to start from scratch. It pulled the plug on my bathtub of worries so I no longer felt the need for self-restraint in front of people.

5:4

I crossed my fingers that it was ready. My typing was out of practice and for the first time the miniature desk in my room was completely cleared of clutter so that I could finish off my degree. The faith from my tutor was a force I had to behold. Straight away he'd given himself as a reference for my master's application. It was the energy I needed to get past all the mental barriers of working remotely, changing the impossible into a manageable challenge in a matter of days. My project title was approved, and I was off. On a laptop that wasn't my own, it remained uncomfortable. I had to really fight to keep my tunnel vision on the work, letting none of my past trauma push my focus away towards the sunny heatwave outside my window. I grabbed the curtain shut, a real twist against my will to step away from the geek's life. But now it was different. I can't be out in public unless I needed supplies and I had to do this to build my road for going forwards. I stared at the computer screen for hours every day. By the time it was over, I felt light-headed. *It's okay.* Now it was summer, and I could prepare to reunite with the outside world again. Interestingly, seeing uni friends again didn't feel too dissimilar to older acquaintances. I hadn't been in contact with them so I worried that they might have thought I didn't care. I was shy to re-emerge in their lives, before my friend baked me a chocolate brownie for my birthday which was as good a welcome back as I could have imagined. Mum got members of the family to see me on a video call while I sat outside the door. Comments flew in about my newly shaved head that was tried out during the indoor period. My housemate had done the same but had live streamed it through the socials. The 'corona cut' would be mostly seen there before it could grow out in time for face-to-face interactions to come back.

Once it sank in that my degree had finished, my position only gathered more pressure to apply for the masters, although it was still unclear when social distancing was going to fade out. Quite a big dilemma emerged without an immediate answer. I was so happy when I bumped into my favourite tutor on the street. He predicted that teaching would be back to normal by the time I'm halfway through the course. Was it worth it for me? I wasn't certain if I could do an MA, let alone at least half of it all remotely. It was a gamble, no doubt about it, but at this point I couldn't see an alternative future. Gut instinct came in again. The application was sent, the laptop placed under a box, family were proud, friends happy to have a housemate for the next year. *Breathe in hope.* Breathe out the strain of my isolating limitations meeting the sheer weight of an online-led world. Safe and secure. I managed to do it with far less hassle than anything else that required me to dip my tool into the oceanic infinity of the sea of connectivity.

It was good to gradually reunite with friends again. The quizzes in the first few weeks didn't seem to matter. We were talking about what we were looking forward to when the time would come, ready to move on from the nothingness we all got to know so well. Internal worries got given some extra space for sympathy across the consensus that we all wanted life to return.

"How am I supposed to live, laugh and love in these conditions?" a friend echoed from TikTok. The influencers had a point there.

5:5

Contradictory and restless, I usually thought about the online world and me in black and white whenever my mood swung in relation to it. I could be ecstatic to see a friend I hadn't seen for months, and yet feel horribly alone, all on the same day. With instant coms palmed off, I couldn't tell one feeling in the grey area from the other. That was the biggest influence on my perception of myself, boiling up with every obstacle or release in all admin and meet-ups. When I was out with a friend, it was nice to hear him say that he didn't need his phone when it died on him. He was sitting next to me, and had reciprocated after I made the decision to go and find him. I was thinking of his own position in advance because he was on crutches from a foot injury and could probably use some company. Knocking on a door brought back childhood memories of someone asking if their friend was free to come out and play. Besides the original reason for my social behaviour being the same, I had grown in confidence enough to do it at twenty-two years old. I wondered if someone was free, and I went up the hill to check directly. The nature of my very sociable house probably persuaded others to do the same. I liked that custom in my village. It would happen without any device in sight. Such a little thing could turn a day around. It meant something significant because of the time put into it after thinking about the performance. Friends were put into action by it.

"It's a sunny day, get up, let's go!" If plans were made days previously, I concluded that there was less of a chance of keeping someone up for it than when I randomly came straight to their door. Think too much about something and you can falter in executing it.

When the pubs reopened in Brighton, something else had entered the fray that I had to learn to bypass. Track and trace. If you tested positive for Covid-19, or someone else who'd been in the venue did, contact would be made to protect people if they wanted to go out and socialise. As I went in first out of a gang of three, I heard my friend snort behind me after a staff member asked if I could write down my phone number on a list, giving my doubts about the moral side of the phone a sharper edge. I hadn't forgotten my number so I ignored the reaction and pretended in front of the staff that it was just a bad joke that wouldn't stop me from getting on with it. As a student, track and trace became more awkward when it turned into an app, with a nemesis barcode at the bar entrance looking like it was taunting me when the line of people in front of it was growing shorter. The weight of potentially missing out on a small social event after being locked away for so long was far heavier than the embarrassment of asking a security guard if pen and paper was an option. They could be cold towards young males in groups, so it could easily feel like you've entered a negotiation table with an intimidating military commander. I was trying to predict if they would tell me to get lost or accept my peculiar terms for getting past them. I sensed a long queue of people behind me, while my mates were already inside. The scenario wasn't any easier to stomach with beer inside of me.

With a gap between the end of my tenancy and getting the keys for my new shared student house coming closer, I was keen to carry on living with friends so that a period of sofa-surfing was about to commence. Everything but a bag of clothes went into my parents' house. My smartphone was no exception. It went into my family's possession as acting secretary while they also had the password to open it. It was mine in principle, but Mum had spent an inordinate amount of money on the unused phone contract. I agreed that this was the best way to handle it until I could access in-person therapy because it was no longer in my responsible (or irresponsible) hands. Seeing as Mum's research had come across a clinic that loosely related to my problem, it wasn't yet available after the first pullback of restrictions because it wasn't strictly a hospital. I wondered if there would be a diagnosis. Blanket terms had been established, but it didn't feel right to park beneath them. Articles on the negative effects of online gaming had been published for a while, but this wouldn't hit the spot. For something everyone my age was using, I believed that I was the only one so I tried to think up my own name for it if that was going to make it into something broader than my own isolated self. At first, I was worrying about where to start. This was my life. Everything I did was influenced by my relationship with the online world in some way. All my friends were coming back to Brighton and reuniting with me, because the online presence of my house was the starting point for it. All my old friends were gone because there was not a single digital point of contact, despite me having bumped into a handful of them on the street. I had no control. The truth about my life and its online associations had been made into a riddle. The place to start was today, but concentration was a battle that would always ensue. I asked myself the question if I really could step into the place of an adequate person.

"Am I good enough?" I murmured, before falling to sleep.

5:6

Tutorials are a significant part of the online world. People narrow it down with food or travel pages, as it offers a plentiful supply if the effort of real life isn't really cutting it.

"I can't be bothered to explain, just look it up online," someone would say. Yeah, let me cycle two miles to the computer cluster at uni to spend ten seconds looking up a recipe for a tofu chow mein. I always had to check myself before asking for tips on things like recipes or playing songs on the guitar. People often told me stuff when it was on the screen and therefore momentarily on their minds. I might have received more information about who said something on Love Island than how to find an exact place I was interested in. It didn't matter what I wanted to know more. And then there were other measures I had to take. Yes, other than dashing from A to B to find a particular person, I've used a fold-out map to navigate, and I use a dictionary and a thesaurus. My trip to the supermarket wouldn't have been as successful without writing down all the items I needed on a scrap of paper. Local seagulls also acted as my alarm clock in the morning. Old fashioned or plain weird, my ways around have deployed whatever resources I had. I needed all the help I could get.

My close friends had gotten used to taking a role in messaging on my behalf, or taking messages from people trying to reach me. It was easy for them, and I suppose they were happy to have the interaction on their smartphones. Then there's people who were taken aback by the effects of this now common occurrence, befuddled when they saw things being put in place when I wasn't using the tech that their lives were propelled by. On the way back to where I was staying, I bumped into my friend who was now back from the Netherlands and doing another year in Brighton, to tell him that his housemate said I could stay at their new place until I got mine.

"Oh! Okay," he replied. Who knows what his dad was thinking of this public interaction out of the blue. We arranged to meet later in the day and I quickly headed back to pack, left a note and a thankyou gift for my vacant friend who had let me use her room for a few nights, and proceeded to wait for my new host to swing by and help me surf over to his sofa. Student life could be so impromptu.

My friends and I were living in the same area for one more year. I was lucky in the way that my village was redesigned. My housemate, having now returned from his year in Canada and living with me once more, told me that his mate needed people in a football team to play in a league at uni, meaning that my crucial points of contact were directing me into my favourite competitive sport. It was all looking eventful, but it was uncertain if another full lockdown was around the corner while the news was glum. I dreaded the thought of doing a whole year studying remotely. Zoom was the classroom where participation and attendance were mutually expected of students.

"Is this what you really want to do?" Mum stressed. "You've got to try the classes if you're doing the course." I replied that I would, but I was aware that my tone didn't sound convincing. As I moved into my new place, it was impossible to remove from the back of my mind that I might have bitten off more than I could chew. I knew I liked what I was going to be studying, once I'd asked a friend to read to me the brief descriptions of my learning modules. All I could do was ride on my passion to get through whatever dirt track my relationship with online education was going to be. When I saw that my timetable had some sessions in a real classroom, I was ecstatic in a way a bedroom worker may never understand. A tutor in the flesh. That was precious and I was going to try and fully get into those seminars because it was an opportunity to feel fully functional in my life.

A new home with housemates I'd lived with before in a student-filled area. It didn't take long until it gathered a reputation as a common room. Tried and tested, the good things hadn't yet come to an end, and it became a part of daily life for me to come home in the evenings and be updated by whoever was in the front room. The custom became far more common than being shown a screen by now, although I felt my phone problem meet my social environment right at the apex when my housemates answered the door to Mum. She wanted me to tell my close friends about everything but I refused point blank. A social dynamic was there. My friends had simply got used to the practical side, and made the banter between us represent how comfortable we had become with each other. They'd known me for long enough now, saying that it increases the excitement of the whole package of catching up when there's no sneak peek on the socials. Someone told me that they had to look twice when they saw me cycling past – they couldn't see me active online so it was like I was literally resurfacing into their world. Bumping into people had that effect on me too. All in all, I loved it. Let spontaneity dictate. I became far more assured about where my feet were standing, warming my hands from the fire of life after getting better at coping with the challenges. I didn't need my friends to understand everything about me to know who I am.

5:7

My tablet was out. The Zoom session was in thirty minutes, but something was missing when I temporarily went back online with a personal device.

"Oh, for crying out loud!" I vented in my closed bedroom. Unable to access the online seminar room, I chucked my tablet under the bed and rushed to my parents' house. *It's okay, I probably needed to use a laptop.* I had my notes ready from the independent work, I was enrolled onto the course to keep my account going. What wasn't I doing that all the students were? My housemate spoke about getting into his Zoom classes like it was nothing. They were really a world apart, weren't they? It wasn't tips they were being asked by me, it was a part of their common sense. I was a half-wit because this was a daily exercise that was easy.

While we were talking, I was quite conscious that there was a chance they'd had this conversation with an elderly relative previously. When I entered a tech store with Grandma to help her choose a new laptop, she was asking me to give her advice on what model to go for, essentially handing me the final decision. Without exaggerating, I was none the wiser.

Fifteen minutes left. I opened Dad's laptop to try the seminar again. Nothing had changed. *Okay, maybe it's because the class hasn't begun yet.* I tried again every minute until it got to 11 am. *Nope, what? And... I'm missing the start of the introductory class, and I haven't identified why.* My parents were suggesting I phone the IT support team at the university. None of this is ever a ten-minute job. I spoke to someone on Mum's smartphone, and they took me though the process step by step, so that the issue could be deciphered. By the end, he concluded that it was fine and it should be working, despite him never tinkering with anything on there.

"If it doesn't work next time, then give us a phone." False start. I had spent over an hour being intensely uncomfortable, and I had achieved nothing. My housemate offered to lend me his laptop for the following week as he hadn't experienced the same difficulty in accessibility. It was the same laptop I'd used to submit my first bit of work at uni before finding out about the computer cluster. I sat at his desk with my notes ready. The whole set up was done by him until he told me how to unmute the mic and left his room.

"I'm so glad you're back from Canada, bro," I added.

It was surreal on the Zoom session. Half the students had their web cams on while I didn't bother in case of any grandad-style, unintended consequences. On the other hand, I wasn't shy since I was genuinely passionate about the topic we were reading about. When going into a small breakout room that was supposed to simulate getting into a group of four, two of the members remained silent, so it was just me and another consulting on the given task.

We asked the other two if they wanted to add anything but the mics were muted. We'll never know. Finishing the seminar, I'd felt that I'd given it a good go, but I began to lose interest in doing things I enjoyed while I was incapable of taking my mind off how to continue navigating through my virtual course. I began to get very stressed and I couldn't focus on coursework. Then there was the weight of expectation that collided with my ongoing struggle to rehabilitate in an online world that demands me to apply my mind to the tasks that looked so easy for people to handle electronically. I was fine! I was fine in the seminar but after a day's lag I was going backwards towards the negativity that brought down my confidence in performing anything for myself. Things got aggravating and anti-social. I thought that the service was designed to be logical and user-friendly, a whole world welcoming me to activate the tools to live as all users do in connection with its interactive matrix.

"You need to compartmentalise it," Mum urged. "Treat it as work, you know, just like using the computer at your uni." Whatever happened, I couldn't separate Zoom classes from my psychological history with the socials. I didn't want to go back there again, but my family were never going to take that well. On the eve of my next online seminar, I decided against attending. These outnumbered the in-person classes eight to one. I was too weak to do it, so I went on to study a masters all on my own. Not to mention I was lying to my family again.

5:8

I couldn't imagine how different people's shopping customs were due to the internet. I've purchased things here and there after dropping my devices because the shops were closed in lockdown so I had to teeter online if my shoes were falling apart. It was reluctant and I would never have sent anything back if it wasn't what I expected, seeing as the potential admin was evaded without a thought. Any habit that brings people to interact gets picked up by the socials. D Pop and the like was becoming a second-hand clothes project for a few of my friends, while the number of people I knew who picked up bargains from Facebook Marketplace seemed to be forever growing. 2 Good 2 Go, an app I'd certainly would have appreciated, was designed to cut out food waste from different eateries by selling things at a discounted price when it would otherwise be thrown out. I'd lost count of the number of times I'd gone for something that cost more financially but with less of a psychological tax in the short run. Online shopping covers everything, another reason that convenience is king. I'd also heard various interpretations as to what crypto currency is valued in the online world. The forms were getting similar attention to how stocks and shares were treated. The activity revolved around the changing speculations of what they're going to be worth. More reasons to go online, more things I had no personal part in besides hearing the thoughts of other people. There were things being developed that I probably didn't have the faintest idea about. It's gone far from where it was before, and it's gone mega-fast.

I found it challenging to comprehend my housemate's sigh when he said, "There's so many group chats at the moment."

"Really?" I responded. Students were excited to do things when social distancing was loosened in Brighton. It was very different to what I was hearing about Manchester, which remained on red alert. Apparently first-year students were literally quarantined in their halls of residence without being allowed to venture out into their initiations into uni life. I couldn't think of anything worse to go through alongside my vicious psychiatric disorder. A blank page can be a very bad place in a way that's easily under-estimated.

I was still going to campus every day to work and I was grateful that friends would join and keep my village lively. My new football league was also on campus, but it was difficult to fit in with a new bunch of lads when I knew that there was a group chat to transfer the money individuals were paying for each individual session. My housemate, who was also in the team, came in again, a part of the lifeline my house had given me in a way I couldn't dream of matching in return. It went a long way when my friend gave me stationery after considering our organizational differences. I made new friends through my already existing ones. When my housemate got 'pinged' on the NHS app telling us all to isolate, a new friend did a supermarket run for all of us while we waited for negative Covid-19 tests results. Supporting each other during an ongoing global crisis could change the meaning of friendship, while it also shifted the way that mental health was being talked about. What had been going on since the first day of lockdown had made people talk of coping with the devilish negativity that can threaten our ability to enjoy ourselves when relative time had slowed everything down after the city's usual activity had stagnated.

Finally, after what seemed like an eternity, I had an appointment in person with a clinical psychiatrist. Not only had the restrictions postponed their availability, but there was also a long waiting list, which indicated that I wasn't alone in preferring face to face. The address for the clinic was quite far out of town and in an area I didn't know. Being clueless as to how long it would take to reach it, my dad lent me an A-Z street map with directions to the clinic marked on there.

I was very nervous on the day. A stranger was about to hear me talk about my torment and make an assessment.

"They're not there to judge you," was one of the last things Dad said to me. My family's decision to make me go private wasn't solely because of specialization or the quality of the service. This was the route to receive in-person treatment when it was still unavailable at the NHS. I needed help, and online communication or phone calls weren't going to work. To receive it earlier, Mum was tempted to ask if they could meet me outdoors, but the wait was over now. I left super-early from my house and walked over there, a journey to the next stage of getting through it all as daylight now faded into dusk. Going towards the unfamiliar was leading me away from all the loss and cold from a previous time. Where would it take me? I would only find out by drifting there.

Part VI

6:1

I was thinking an awful lot about where to begin. It's pretty much a life story, but in my head it sounded all incoherent and jumbled up. With my dad's A-Z in my hands, I paced along a main road while checking the door numbers of the buildings to my right. What is this clinic going to look like? A pang of nerves hit me when I walked past a chiropractor's clinic. *That wasn't it, but maybe it would look alike.* The numbers crept closer to the one matching the address and I realised I was speeding up to find it sooner and cut down the time for anxiety. There it was, within a large, white-walled house, with a small car park situated before it. The sun had set by now and the lampposts flicked on. As I looked at the trees around the site, the thought of frightened rabbits entered my mind as an automatic door opened in front of me. Inside the lobby round the corner was a receptionist sat down with a face mask on, looking up and greeting me with a half-question.

"You're fine."

"Don't worry."

"I wouldn't overthink it." You see a smile that suggests you're being silly. The incomprehension undermines its reality. A short motivational speech is assumed to make it all vanish, when really it adds acidity to the sting of having a huge part of you separated from the emotional experience they claim to understand. It brought me down further. No one I knew could possibly have understood my problems, which is why I'd gone to this clinic to see someone with the qualifications to assess what was making me feel the way I did.

"I'll let him know you're here. If you would like to sit in the waiting room, please," the receptionist politely directed me. I sat alone in there, feeling my legs go numb, waiting to be summoned by a new person who was about to hear it all. Accompanied with my thoughts, I'd left the winter darkness to adjust my eyes to the bright lights of the clinic's interior. Soon, a man poked his head in the doorway and asked for me and I quickly got up to follow him, both of us with face masks as legislated at the time. When I reached an upstairs room with him, my imagination of a fictional portrayal of a psychiatrist's office was met by a similar aesthetic. It was comfortable. I was offered a seat in a soft armchair placed next to a low table with a box of tissues. Once the doctor took his seat opposite me, I was totally relieved to be given permission to take off my face mask while he also did the same. Face-to-face it turned out to be. He began by repeating what Mum had said to the practice over the phone while inviting me to add bits for myself. I then went into the whole story starting from my early teens and he was jotting down on his notepad. He kept nodding as I heard my voice come out in a way it never had before, letting me ignore the squiggle of his pen. I lost myself in it, flying through time right up to the present day, but with zero expression coming out of the monotone narration as if I was articulating a deep confession. I realised that he could see my position quite quickly, phrasing the next questions in a way that got me talking from the abyss that was until now unexplained. The doctor heard other young people mention the socials with their difficulties. As for the mobile phone, he appreciated that the modern day had seen it fused with the computer in miniaturised form. There were also questions about my general health, such as the history of mental health in my family, and lifestyle. The session was extensive. He wanted to hear a lot from me, but at the end, the treatment plan he presented felt a little underwhelming at first. It was to be split into two halves, the first being a cognitive-behavioural therapy program that I couldn't receive in person yet until restrictions were further loosened (Their therapy team weren't classed as medical professionals). The second half was medication. I didn't know what my view was on taking pills, but if that was the only thing available right away then I was failing to see what it would change.

"You seem ... disappointed," the doctor said. In my position, I was eager to try whatever it takes, so I pulled through my doubts over the effectiveness of prescribing me drugs. If it was going to tinker with my mind to prevent it from dropping into severe depression then sure, perhaps it would give me the space I needed to work out how I was going to get better. The doctor praised that I'd come out and told my family, and for having a strong friendship circle that I'd managed to maintain without being directly contactable on their terms. A lot of his patients weren't so lucky with personal support despite me having lost a lot in all the frenzy. Meanwhile, the diagnosis from the doctor was very curious. He had put different things out loud to suggest the combinational element of my condition, but the conclusion was left to my final say in what it was that he was approaching as a doctor. I denied that it was a phobia, saying I wanted to use the phone again in a way that was safe. My tales of gingerly holding my smartphone with the screen faced away from me like it was an unexploded bomb, were a result of the associations that my brain had developed with it. I needed the phone to live. That's why I hadn't thrown it off Brighton pier or anything. The hazards were there, so the doctor introduced the term graded exposure to me. In this case, that meant steadily adopting the barebones functions of a mobile so that I could grow more comfortable with the object itself. And that was the goal I found myself setting in front of him.

Being prescribed sertraline would numb me to the nastier thought patterns that had been plaguing me. In theory, that would allow the best chance of tackling the central problem. After two hours, I came out of the session utterly drained of energy and ravenous for food, so I walked back home and came back from the inside of my mind. An appointment was booked with the doctor in a month's time along with my prescription. Treatment was happening now for real. That internal predicament that had been touched under everything people knew about me was out of the fog that engulfed my whole perception of myself, coming to grasp the place that I occupied but had not known what to call. Now I could see the ground where I was standing.

I knew very little about anti-depressants. There were none that I could name before I was prescribed sertraline but I was quite aware that it was a big decision that's not right for everyone experiencing mental health problems. Once tried, there's always the chance that it could make things worse, but for me this was not the case. The dose was scheduled to steadily increase, while it wasn't only depression that the meds were treating, but several symptoms that were produced by my mind's relationship with the digital stratosphere. The nausea and the bizarre sensation of my mood bouncing back up in the first few days were miniscule once it had entered my system and put my head back on its shoulders. I was purposeful, and getting more confident in a very short space of time, making my friendships flourish from the buds of comradery to fully flowered independent connections. Potential stigma or shame didn't hold me back from expressing myself any longer. Freedom became much more translatable to my entire nervous system. And best of all, the huge changes in my mental life didn't make me forget the meaning of a self-hood that I had locked away for years, smoothly transferring away from the isolated withering of my core as I contemplated that cliff drop without seeing much to gain by pulling myself back in the opposite direction. The grass looked greener, and my experience inspired my passion to help the people in my life leave nothing unsaid that covers the emotional conflicts that take place beneath their skin. I don't blame anyone for my long silence in the slightest, but I don't want any silence on something so big to be tremendously long like my own. I wouldn't wish that on anyone.

6:2

The smartphone was a whole world in their hands. I simply couldn't afford to see it as my enemy. It was a tool used for so many things, and not carrying one had left some people with the impression that I wouldn't use other technologies.

"Of course, Luke's got cash on him," I heard my mate say behind me at a bar, as he got his Apple Pay out. I enjoyed joking about the socials, since if I continued to be bitter about them, then I would never feel healthy next to them. It became safe for me to be around people using them so I shouldn't cause a fuss when they do. It's a big deal for people, because they receive most of their info from the tool so there's often going to be content on their feeds that I'm interested in too. The more I tried to understand the socials as a big feature of people's lives, the less threatening it started to feel after the damage I did to myself as a child. That was how I improved at connecting with all the people around me who use it. Talk of it shows that it's a part of an individual life itself, and it was still a part of mine too. I couldn't cancel that.

A key part of the smartphone is its memory. Anything posted online is recorded and leading to alerts that represent an action from the tip of a finger that is far from a one-off. Music, for example, is listed by customization while stream services guess what you could be looking to hear from an intelligent search bar that displays stylistic parallels to what is observed from its listeners. It makes additional content instantly accessible. The music is all there, so you don't have to rack your brains for that tune you can't quite remember the name of. AI DJing can read what the listener likes – all the creative work is already done. My friend said to me that her mum was impressed that I was stringing up songs on someone-s smartphone during a birthday celebration without a pre-prepared playlist to help me. The friend answered that it was because I didn't usually have a smartphone doing it for me, so it made my brain prepare to remember songs to pull out on the spot.

I'd long given up on getting fed up with people saying, "How have you not seen this? I'm so surprised!" Most of the new shows on Netflix will only last a little while before they are replaced by others in people's memory. But seeing as some programs are only around on the service for a limited amount of time, you'd have to really commit to get through an entire series that runs for hours if you want to say you've watched it. It's often futile to suggest letting it go when there's so much to see on offer. Lockdown presented a window, but a few months of it wasn't enough to complete everything what people brand as a must-see. The next episode plays unless you pick up the controller and manually close it. It's effortless to binge away.

No wonder that my own free time can feel like a long time.

Things don't always go according to plan. That's life, but a situation like this used to be enough to make me panic. I didn't have an easy way of chopping and changing an arrangement. I would stretch myself to my limits to ensure that something went ahead, to prevent the recurrent thoughts from coming back to add their tally to the panic attack chart. But as I noticed my treatment coming into effect, this black and white narrative no longer acquired such a powerful place. One morning, I left half an hour before an appointment to find that the front wheel was missing from my bike. It was too late to walk or work out which bus route would get me to the clinic. I had no Uber, no phone either – no appliance to manage my way around this emergency. I still decided I couldn't miss the appointment. Everything was all lined up and the only factor letting it down was on my side of the fixture. I had to make it. Turning my back on the bike wreck, I nipped back home and quickly changed into my running gear. Not knowing the time on route, I ran for it. I ran for my mental health and arrived in the nick of time to recover my breath. *Breathe in… and out. In…*

"Morning, Luke." My doctor poked his head round the doorway and I followed him up again, wiping the sweat off my forehead. I had made it, and another appointment began.

"How are you?" It wasn't for a few months that I'd see someone from the clinic's therapy team, but it felt like narrating it all did a whole deal of good. The doctor said that he had friends who didn't use a mobile, but this didn't cut them off from being contactable without depending on their family or housemates. He kept assuring me that I hadn't really dropped off. I'd only taken something away that made me miss out on potential things. I could book appointments in person when I was there, and I could hand repeat prescription slips to receive my meds. That doesn't sound unconventional now, does it? The doctor was probing at angles to reintroduce a contact device of some kind into my life.

"I take it your aim is to use a mobile again?"

"Yes, I think so, given that I'm finishing uni next year," I answered. So far, there was no resolution other than taking part in a call on loudspeaker between two other friends.

"Okay, you're not ready yet. We're just waiting for therapy to be allowed in person." He picked an individual for me, saying that he would be very frank and get down to the nitty-gritty of the issue. I've had several appointments by now. I wasn't afraid, and the doctor could tell how hard I was trying now that my general wellbeing had dramatically improved.

"Keep doing what you're doing and things will get better," he promised. I took those words with open arms. Since our first meeting, my commentary had become more expressive, going as far as ending with a laugh as I gave an example of when I rocked up to a friend's place to see them open their door with wide eyes.

"Oh, hey Luke! What you doing here?"

"I just came to say 'hey'. Fancy some food?" I had to revel in the randomness in my appearances back into someone's world, when on the contrary I wasn't a direct part of their pocket one that usually throttled their social life into ignition.

6:3

"How are you financing these appointments?" my doctor asked.

"My parents," I replied.

"Right, how do you feel about that?"

"Guilty," I said thoughtlessly. The cost of private treatment was now thrown into the mix of the original feelings of shame. It was my mess that I'd gotten into, and now the Bank of Mum & Dad had to be called, while my conscience remained unsettled. The triple figures for every session provided another reason for me to wave my finger at myself. As a student working a part time job, I couldn't afford to finance it all independently. Plus, I had no idea how long it would all take. I'd thought of everything yet easing my way back to a phone didn't have a safe crossing. The tenancy with my housemates wasn't going to last forever.

Later in the term I had three weeks of classes with my favourite offline tutor once again, and I realised how much I'd missed his style. In-person teaching with a whiteboard was back, and it was in a room with the biggest one I've ever seen. It was also good to finally return the books he'd lent me right before the first lockdown. Now I finally had the chance. At the end of a seminar, it was the definition of bittersweet when I was talking with a course mate about the upcoming essay, putting into perspective one of the best perks of learning after failing to take part in the online classes. The motivation coming from passionately sharing ideas was a key contribution to the best graded pieces of work I did on the course. I'd missed out on a lot; I knew I did. My decision to carry on with the course didn't come without the emotional tax.

I'd come to terms with the fact that it was common knowledge in my social environment that I wasn't using a phone, but when my friend's housemates were approaching me, they looked fascinated.

"You don't have a phone. That's so cool!." They barely knew me, but I didn't get stressed. I laughed at the remark and thanked them for the compliment. I wasn't embarrassed. I was almost proud at times that I'd been able to get this far without using it. Bumping into a school friend who asked me for my number if I wasn't on the socials, I sort of gestured that a number wasn't available either.

"You're so low-key!" he exclaimed. I let him take a selfie of us to send to a friend who'd apparently talked about me in a group chat after I approached him in the supermarket. My separate mental worlds were making more sense to me, so their crisscrossing didn't pull away at my brain like it used to. Everything became clear so I didn't feel myself shrink in the nervous anticipation that I'd have to engage in something where I'd stagger on the spot.

"You know you're the only one," a newer friend put in earnest. The harrowing back story didn't prohibit an answer from me anymore. Opening out was always going to lead to a happier outcome, but I only truly appreciated that once I'd evolved to influence my identity from my deliberate digital divide. My friends were posting me letters (some of them anyway) regarding a change of plan or a private message, and I made sure to return them. My village was close-knit and I decided that some of the characters I'd met at uni brought me so much joy that I jokingly asked them for an autograph to pin up in my kitchen. Making fun out of my relations with other people when they couldn't text me seemed to work in displaying goodwill towards my heroes. I didn't want them to ever shy away from expressing their quirks to me as a friend. Before that year, a part of my humanity was impalpable in a way that drove me to try and help the people in my life get away from the shadows if it made them more comfortable in being themselves without any need to pretend. If a friend honoured me with their trust offline, I zealously looked after it because my young mind valued the connection when I was lacking it in conventional terms. It mattered to my heart because I was feeling more like a part of a network without using the easiest tool available to build it.

6:4

Tons of people don't bother exchanging phone numbers, because the socials do that and loads more besides, almost all on a single app. It's the point where they can all meet without having to move their bodies into action, and it felt like everything could be initiated there. Some will find it more powerful than themselves over their own lives, so there's always a chance that the displays that push into people's faces might be aggravating when a person's behaviour only needs to be a little wrong in someone else's eyes for their mood to alter. It can take such a big place in the mind that it's hard not to let it slide away.

The winter lockdown was bleak. It challenged the mental wellbeing of a large demographic as there didn't appear to be much excitement ahead. There was so much spare time. If someone lived alone, or was finding a housemate rather difficult, the additional company was happily received. A walk and a takeaway coffee in a pair became the public social activity of the season. Friends committed to a time and a place, seeing as they didn't have much else to do. Brighton was transformed by its bars and restaurants being closed for business. Helping your neighbour when they were isolating was a way of forming lasting friendships, as was the case when my housemate helped next door. A couple of months later, a bunch of them would frequently see me at work and give my shifts a wider sense of community in an offline life that continued to benefit from the rawness of my experience of locality. But a little while after, one of them expressed concern in a humorous manner as to what they would do if I went missing. I looked at her with a grin on my face before she answered her own question. She'd go up to the garden centre. The decision out loud made me teasingly nod in agreement. If I really did go missing, I'm sure that there was a higher chance that it would be game over. Well, I'd hate to say it to someone who cared about me, but that was a chance I was willing to take.

Mum was trying to comprehend what professional help was going to mean in terms of how long it would be until my family could contact me. She then told me that my uncle suggested that I should get a pager. A pager! I couldn't picture what this was at the time, but I later realised that I'd used one before when awaiting a food order at the student bar. The idea of it didn't make my mental wall give way however, as I insisted that any personal device would ultimately have the same effect on me, given that the association of contact in my head was the factor in play. Before long, Mum was asking how long my treatment was going to go on for and when it was predicted that I would break away from my impractical equilibrium.

"What is the treatment plan or strategy?"

"If I don't bloody know, then how is he going to?!" I snapped,

"It's not like treating a broken leg!" I reacted like a landmine to the conversation, forgetting that the question was coming from a good place that was also paying for the whole thing. I wished it was a broken leg... official therapy couldn't come sooner.

I worked to improve my communication skills because exchanging zero texts on my own accord was literally keeping me on my toes, practicing, exploring, and suddenly being treated as someone different from the person I was only a short while before. A climatic example of this took place leading up to Christmas. My friends had gifted me a brick, burner phone which touched every deeper feeling inside me towards connectivity and having support from people on the other side of it. They told me that they would love a call or a text on Christmas Day, but more importantly, a means of contact when uni was all over. The idea of a simple non-smartphone was thrown about by everyone and it did bring out that huge question: did I want to carry one for myself? I wasn't always stopping at yes or no, being unable to see a harmless outcome from solely focusing on either of the two without making them blend into a concoction of complications. Nonetheless, I was watching my friend add the numbers of people who cared about me with a smile on his face, while I listened to another reading how to activate the SIM. The gesture momentarily pushed aside the question when my mates were sat around me making the effort to engage with an issue totally separate from their everyday lives and its challenges. There was the slightly awkward downer that such a small, simple, everyday object was plain unhealthy for me to carry, but the warmth and purity around the act hit me in a much more unforgettable way that would define the moment in my memory. It was that part that led me into sacrificing some security in my mental health to send at least a text message to a few friends at Christmas, with my sister acting as scribe. The season's greetings were sent through my smartphone, seeing as that was already set up. I got it done and dusted in the morning to try and give them something at least. I guessed that situation was the line where non-conformity would make me feel that I was betraying my heroes. Sadly, most heroes gain the title by performing acts you can't do yourself. I told my family not to let me know about any replies, but Mum wasn't having it.

"Look, one of them's replied to you! Don't you want to see his message?" My subconscious squirmed at the apprehension of the floodgates releasing a revival of head-filling discomfort. It was seeking to prove that one thing always led to another. I didn't want the scorching flames of it to envelope me and cut away with razor-sharp precision as I felt my protective measures being taken away. Too late. The family get-together was almost spoiled for me by an explosion of rage erupting from my foul tongue as my vocal cords trumpeted my lack of control over the device that, I knew more than anything, had been clasped in a way more harmful than its architects could possibly imagine. I yelled at Mum with fury after she read my friend's festive reply aloud with innocent glee. I had created a world for myself. Under the rule of user-friendly networks in the external one, my online world was a minefield that could be set off no matter which direction I go towards an interaction through it in the normal way. It's easy to see I wasn't very welcome in this world.

6:5

"Get your calculator out. It won't do the discount automatically." I interrupted my colleague who was serving at the next till, and asked if I could borrow their smartphone. They quickly tossed their phone on my desk so that I could do the sum. My manager then later asked me to replenish a shelf to fill the gaps where products had gone.

"If you take a picture on your phone, you can see at the back which stock can go out." How could I refuse? I wasn't going to say to the big cheese that I wouldn't do this straightforward task. I ran to the till and took some receipt paper and a pen, squiggling at top speed to race through the long way round. I had to work the extra mile to make sure none of my superiors thought I was incompetent. The semi-lockdowns gave me a new appreciation for my job at the garden centre as other things were yet to physically reopen. Working remotely was a legacy of social distancing that ended up staying in effect. People wanted to stick with it once they grew into the habit, but I was glad that the walkie-talkie in the garden centre was the closest thing to it on my end. Meanwhile, I was intrigued at what some of my newer companions were making of my position. Friends were mentioning it to their folks and their thoughts were shared with me.

"Did you find him in the street?" my mate's mum asked when a selfie was sent to her of us both. A lot of the time that was spot on.

"He has beliefs no one would ever understand," another said. I didn't really mind walking under a ladder, and my coppers had never sunk at the bottom of a public fountain. I would have been less secretive as to why I'd refused to carry a mobile or use the socials if it was to do with principle. The short answer was that I didn't trust my view on mobile communication, but I formed trust in people who use it. They'd kept me going, so I was relying on the socials as much as a lot of people, albeit in a more randomly selective way. In other words, luck played a part, both good and bad. I also didn't think that Steve Jobs' passing was fake news, and that his brain was in a fluid container somewhere pressing buttons with some robotic arms. I was unwell, and a single sentence from me led to more questions, not an indication that people had been provided with an answer they'd understand. There was a pang of irritation brushing me when Dad referred to it as a phobia. Mum named it a full-blown disability once she'd processed that there were a lot of things I couldn't do.

Grandma looked at me after I tried to describe my pain to her, "It's only an object." Bless her heart, she'd always get any salve or plaster for all the cuts and bruises I picked up as a child, but talking about the devastation that governed my life led her to respond that a device is a simple unit that shouldn't be bigger for the human brain. The online world was what for many characterised how far everything's advanced since the neolithic age in human history, yet some things about humanity will always remain the same. It's easy to forget how close to the chimpanzee we are.

Here we go. I've gone to the same clinic, but not to meet the familiar face of my doctor. I was due to tell the story again to a new face. The therapist was really looking for details, behaving in a friendly manner that showed a devotion to improving the health of his patients. He shared personal experiences as a recovering alcoholic and the treatment that brought him out of the pit he'd left behind. Like the doctor, he wanted to equate my issue with an eating disorder, whereby there was a harmful relationship with said object, but it was needed to survive so my brain had to be re-tuned to it. He told me that a professional theorised to him a while back that his issues were like a disease, although he later had the analogy adjusted to an allergy instead. Fair enough. I liked thinking of my issue as an allergy. It connected it to reality in a clearer way. Wow, words do wonders. Everyone needs protein to survive, but give peanuts to the wrong person, and it could be deadly. Everyone needs social contact, but give me a smartphone, and I would lose the plot.

I'd also completed another form that assessed the general nature of my mental health on paper. Upon reflection, it was unsurprising that I was over-eating and over-sleeping. I was leading an active life, and taking turns between my housemates to cook dinner for everyone which inserted healthy meals, but I didn't know when to stop and chill out. My brain got burnt out so the longer average night sleep was a part of the end of my difficulty in keeping still, not to mention with the amount of coffee that I was drinking. I was a fidget and a gannet, forgetting my need to rest until I grew more irritable and stressed. My mind raced a lot faster than my body in applying itself to some plan I'd made three days previously until a disjunction filled me with frustration. People were snapped at; friendships were tested. I tried to keep a level head and a busy life, but sometimes I wouldn't know when to make it less complicated than rocket science. It makes it easy for me to wear and tear. I needed to sit and chat with anxiety instead of always thinking about how I could distract my animal from taking care of me. A consultation with it would make my worries over contact simmer down so that they weren't so much alike with when I was using the socials to try and endear the young people around me. I didn't do well at that so leave it be. That would furthermore make a phone, separate from this social code, feel unconnected to the devil on my shoulder trying to persuade me to feed a compulsion for reassurance. It's okay to do nothing when that gives the amount of rest required to face your own difficulties. It would take a considerable fraction of my entire life to improve at that.

I was grateful for the printouts of advice about addressing intrusive thoughts and the tug of war to push them out. For distress would renew itself when I was faced with personal devices, so now I had a published list of tactics to read and use to prevent my mind responding in a way that encourages a bigger spot of bother. I noticed some similar ideas to what friends of mine had mentioned on other occasions, whether they were influenced by their own counselling sessions, or their studies at university. Saying the names of objects in your field of vision can be effective in grounding yourself in thinking clearer. I hadn't read much psychology, but my treatment had an educational factor that I grew to value highly. When I went on a slight tangent in mentioning that occasionally I'd given into temptation to search up something at my leisure on the uni PCs, the slight regret I felt from it when it scraped my triggers prompted my therapist to describe it as 'interesting' rather than a cause for concern about a possible additional mistake. I wasn't shooting myself in the foot, but it was a relevant feeling to be noted so that it would be less panic-inducing and prickly in the future. This was in enormous detail, but talking about it helped me understand that it was needed as far as these small, everyday elements added up to the bigger picture.

6:6

"Oh, it's you who doesn't have the phone!" someone said to me upon the first time properly chatting. Word had spread everywhere. People were shy to express their shock, but as they got to know me, it arrived.

"How do you even live? I literally can't leave my house without my phone."

"I'm still alive," I blankly declared.

"Are you, like, completely off the grid?" someone else guffawed. If we're getting into that side of things, then I still have a registered bank account. I had to play dumb sometimes when the sincerity element grew. I was much more appreciative of being humanised.

"It's who you are. When you speak to Luke, it's Luke." It was maverick, but the part that made me feel calmer about the comments was that people viewed a face-to-face conversation to be inviting more honesty than an exchange of messages. It represented more of what I wanted for myself: to fully associate with the world again in a way that was safe. The question was: could I see the difference between safety and unnecessary caution?

There was a lot of time to fill. Contrary to predictions, the second term of the year was held online, and the mood that followed could only be addressed by a willingness to step into adventure within any means available. This helped me in some ways, because friends made the effort to step outside the box. They continued to meet me at a specific time and place for a walk, as a lot of restless energy could be allotted to moral support without always needing a phone on my end. The benefits of my village remained at full strength and when someone asked if I wanted to do a month-long running challenge, it was impossible to decline. A handful of us, including one of my housemates, let Strava on someone's phone measure the distance covered on the go, significantly letting users validate that the run took place with a finish time for the set number of miles.

"If the run's not on Strava, then the run didn't happen," I quipped, as my mate worried that it didn't record our run for the day. A photo was uploaded at the end of each consecutive one, going up a mile everyday with sporadic rest days to remember that Strava didn't make any of us immortal. The smartphone as a tool was used by me, even if multiple Stravas had measured a length differently to one another and sparked a debate between my friends over the exact mileage. What I found especially motivating was hearing how many minutes each individual mile took to complete, making me want to push myself harder. Strava was a social, and people want their success to be seen by all their followers. As our slightly ludicrous challenge was reaching near to the end, we took five days off to rest our joints from the hard impact of the concrete surfaces. Like with any need I had that was a little bit niche, I always hoped that this store or that had what I was looking for before I'd concede that I had to look online. My knee was injured and I wanted to get an elasticated support to hold off the worst. A game of chance ensued, but I found one. If only I could have phoned in to book leave from work so that we could have followed tradition to do the marathon on a Sunday.

Instead, I'm doing it on a Saturday with a seven hour shift the next day. The inconveniences all added up, but this marathon was for my friends.

"Don't forget Strava though," I laughed, as my friends made a mental note before we set off. Two of them liked to have their AirPods in while running; I was declaring a lengthy assault against any mean flashback that presented itself to me. One time in my first year, I had trained with my housemate before in preparation for his official marathon. We did some long runs, although the idea of doing it myself was thwarted by the online admin. I was full of doubt, until now. I had the social trapeze I needed to get on the platform to make me do it. It was also a lot of fun, having this sociable day out, and having friends prepare a pit stop halfway in. I told my family about the challenge beforehand, but I hadn't seen them for a week, so I wondered if they would come out to the finish. At a certain point with my mate beside me, I asked to borrow his phone and dialled my parent's landline, as we continued to pace ourselves well into the challenge.

"Hello?" Mum's phone-voice answered in my ear, for the first time in an eternity.

"Hi Mum. I'm just doing the marathon. Would you like to get to the finish for 3 pm?" I guessed the rough time. Later, I was dashing along what I thought was the home stretch, seeing my friends appear closer and closer at what should have been the finish line, but then my friend was calling my name ten meters behind me, telling me we had to do a further half a mile lap around the park. I'd already turned up the gas. A psychological cyclone swept through me after being informed that there was more to go when I thought I was only meters away from completing a marathon. When we'd completed the extra distance, Strava apparently claimed that we hadn't quite finished, but my legs were like lead. I had a suspicion that my very competitive friend may have called the extra lap to catch me up in front of our spectators. I'll never know; at that point I didn't care. I was elated and my family soon arrived to see me. I lost myself in a way I'd forgotten was possible. Everything I'd lived for became crystal clear. I later told my friend that it was one of the best days of my life for that reason alone, even if that title didn't take much to gain. Handed the rope, I was clambering out of the deep, dark pit that had engulfed me in shadows, moving out there and taking responsibility in the real world while it's been dominated by its digital nodes. Mum told the rest of my family and apparently members were in utter disbelief.

"Well, you have to do the real one now, don't you?" she commented. For all my obstructions, what I'd done that winter was a stepping stone to the official event in six months' time.

"We'll apply for you," Mum reassured me, before I could hesitate. If I knew I could do it, my 'secretaries' would set it up. A fundraiser could be set up too. I didn't have to think about which charity to run for. I was going to take on the challenge once more that year for the mental health support charity, MIND.

6:7

When I saw people huddled together, it felt like there was a whole connected world shifting around me with its arrangements being the portal to all offline things. My housemates and my wider village were great, but when walking down the street in my own company, it sometimes took some energy to shrug off the delusion that everyone around me knew something I didn't while they were connected. The place where it's all organised and entangled moves in ways unknown to me until the sharp edges of people's communication overtake all that I'd previously managed to find out. I thought that I should have always been doing something or else I've not done enough at all. Meet someone, or become totally behind what has updated a huge portion of minds on how they manage their relations with every desire their compass points to. At moments, I was quite powerless unless I found more space to move; space that's been squeezed tighter and tighter by all the growing reasons to go online that widens the gap between me and the others. My path off course from the convenient avenues towards the things that make a life feel more whole often diverge them away while I potentially feel useless and unwanted, incapable of doing something right just because I couldn't do the one thing that people turn to without thinking. I wasn't alone as a person with problems exacerbated by online life, but I was incapable of connecting online with anyone else with whom I could share them. My radar was limited, so my attention was left to those I already knew. My doctor told me directly that it was right for me to stay off social media for the rest of my life. I struggled to reimagine the speed and superfluidity of it all.

The chances were that the next person I spoke to would have felt better if I communicated to them in a comfortably organic way. The one thing I was conscious of was that I couldn't do it with my own slick vehicles for transmission, so I had to make any communication count. Since I wasn't tapping a touchscreen at will, I couldn't afford to dilute an interaction with easy lines or non-meaningful gestures, seeing as it was going to take considerable effort to stick with a plan with someone, while there was already an online network that was designed to reach as many people as you liked. If people could get back to me in a way in which I wasn't squashed into the same old situation of aggressive negativity, then that was a precious gift that was going to help me beat depression. In the world we lived in, a lot of work was required to make that understood by the people in my life. Diplomacy is something an individual subconsciously puts energy into when they go through maturity. The non-stop rhythm of online life didn't convince my core to abandon that aspect of humanity regardless of being so off-kilter to this stage for connectivity. Friends were more than happy to text for me, evidently feeling that it was a social interaction on their device that would make them feel good anyway. I thanked them for it, sometimes feeling bad that I was asking them to give their time to be the one in the middle. But it appeared to be no hassle. Not ever. It's on their fabric so it takes no brain power unlike with learning something or solving a problem. If someone, however, was trying to plan something with me alone then I could see from their facial expressions that it counted as work.

"Who will you be with? I'll text them." The network they used every day had its designers developing it to build on what was already there, with the idea that good marketing would occur when the user appreciated some new feature. Users were a part of the process, so when my friends applied themselves to working out something that was outside the margin of user-friendly computer science, I knew there was meaning to it. They weren't just lying in bed, typing a message within seconds. I had to appreciate they were doing a lot more than that to be my friend. I could never be thankful enough.

A bigger and better computer cluster at uni was enough to reshape my village. More and more of my friends were attracted by the dual monitors in a bigger space. I was only stunned I hadn't gone there earlier in my studies. A day on campus could feel like a day at work, and there was always someone to join for lunch. It was a friend's recommendation that finally brought me there. He'd spent hours there every week, but was also easily distracted. He liked doing a lot of different things all at once, so focusing on a single task for a length of time was no easy task. It was a perfect disposition for the online world to swamp his hyper-ventilated habits. I think he liked having me there to try and counter-balance the easy swing towards his phone. He'd brought in a chess set to replace the online world for his breaks, and I was content to let him thrash me if that was going to help him handle something I avowedly sympathised with. On another day, he asked me to confiscate his phone while we were in the cluster. Regardless of my own history, I complied, not knowing how much of a test this would be for him. After about an hour, his friend sat next to him and told him about a way to do well on crypto for a limited time only. Having been commanded by the captain of the university rugby team to hold on to his phone no matter what, I firmly said no when he asked for it back to engage with e-commerce. In monetary terms, I didn't have a clue what was being talked about and my self-restraint was never going to waver with my own devices so ultimately, keeping another's away from them was going to have the same result.

"Give it back. I need it!" he barked. "Where is it? It's my phone!" I didn't grasp how serious this was to him, having been a world apart from the whole thing while knowing all too well how to hide it away.

"That's a shame," I taunted him in ignorance. The phone still didn't move when his close friend accused me of loving the power. When my mate got up and approached me menacingly, it only made me tell him off for not getting on with his essay.

Eventually he lost his temper, "For fuck's sake, you made me lose 300 quid, you prick!" I couldn't have pictured the logistics behind the numbers. Returning his phone back to him late in the afternoon, I found him upstairs playing chess with a friend and I tried work out if he was genuinely annoyed with me. Was I stubborn or headstrong? Or didn't it matter in the end? Whatever it meant to him, I accepted his initial request in full, and apologised for how I interpreted it, not really knowing how to feel about the day. I didn't think afterwards that the absence of his phone made any difference to his work rate. If anything, it made it worse, leaving him stressed within the hour of his sharp withdrawal. A gadget where whole lives are organised is a lot of invisible power until you feel you've lost it, and it seems very heavy. My agitated friend told me upon getting to know me, that he hated the smartphone, so I could never have anticipated the extent it would hit him when he's barred from his personal virtual life for a day. I should have known better. My own relationship with the online world felt at its worse for a while after barring myself rather than when I engaged with it. Was it narcotic like that? Could taking it away really feel like the end of the world? It's a very powerful thing indeed.

6:8

"You know he doesn't even have a phone," one of my colleagues said to another, right in front of me.

I pretended to be confused. "What? How could anyone possibly live without a phone?" The grapevine became uncertain as their befuddled faces looked at me.

"Of course, I have a phone!" I wasn't lying, but those remarks didn't oblige me to show and tell so I walked on and carried on with my day. It was even better when someone was shocked at how I was up to date with someone's social life.

"How do you know? You don't even have a phone!" I simply replied that I asked them. There were different perspectives. Some commented that you needed to phone your mum from time to time. If I missed out on a meet-up then it sometimes warranted a snide remark that if I had a phone, I would have known what was going on.

Others would perform something on their smartphone before following it with a gloating remark.

Something like, "This is what you can do on a smartphone!" *Thanks for the fresh insight. Really appreciate it. Thanks.* There could be borderline tension from the extent to which my position was challenging minds. But I was less ashamed of it now. I'd come to understand myself better, and I was witnessing my friends doing it differently for me when they wanted to. With all this help, most days did leave me feeling like I could genuinely co-exist, confident in front of people that the difficulty in processing the tangible outcome of my issue doesn't make me assume the next time around that someone is right to show distaste in any way they want. One comment would no longer pierce my skin to the point where I needed to hide away. I felt stronger than the shadow I was before, going up to that staff member in the supermarket instead of the self-checkout. No anxiety in making eye contact; no effort in gliding from my dissociated state to talking to a stranger in public. I wasn't only fine at the time. I was happy that I could do one of many of the little things that helped me realise my personality without the socials. I wasn't the only one who appreciated a reason to do something offline either, but I never want to come across as someone who thought they were above the people who were active on the socials. In fact, I began to value calling someone a friend who had a big online presence. I'd rather be an ally than not. It was always an extension of human beings who should be respected without preaching to everyone to stay off the socials because they're not good for anyone. It was clear that people around me could be capable of bringing it back to its use value by stripping back pointless distractions. That's one of many ways to make cyber-relations healthier in mental terms. I know I've benefited from seeing friends finding employment through the socials, whether it's a free drink at a promotional event, or earning cash at a friend's outdoor cinema. I also found it entertaining in expressing that: *actually, I am here existing in your newsfeed, even if I have no account for you to follow!* I no longer had the fierce animosity I carried earlier on at uni, learning that I didn't get better from brewing hatred inside of me. Though I was glad not to be a part of giving domestic pets an online profile to share their pictures. Obviously, pets are special to their owners and the number of likes is a way people check to prove it. But Pesto doesn't want an Instagram account. Yes, he might be transfixed by the wild birds on BBC's *Springwatch,* or he might enjoy gift-wrap skiing across the carpet, but my family don't need to publicise that for me to find it hilarious. Pesto's not going to know who's following the perfect moments in his life. The online world gives everything a place in people's heads, but Pesto remains unfazed where the contents of his bowl is concerned.

My thought patterns quickly became less self-alienating as I found that other people have felt similar to me towards online life: the worries over something happening without our part in it, the desire for satisfying a standard social ID that still distinguishes yourself from everyone else, the inward-looking measurements of success that fill your time and brain with the data that can change it. I found that knowing no one who'd dropped it all and had experienced the emotional implications of leaving behind a heavy online past, didn't separate me from everyone de facto like I once assumed. The socials play into people's nature; that's why masses of people want to use it. But having a decent conversation with fellow members of my generation did inform me that my position does make sense at a practical level, and it certainly doesn't separate between me and my friends the mutual feeling of togetherness that can lead to good times and support for one another. Feeling that way between me and another person, regardless of my non-electro extremes, had become the proudest part of my life as a young person. It was that which made me want to look after myself and overcome the incessant challenge of living my life offline at a time when it is far too easy to believe that this is impossible. If the conversation is possible, then the rest can stand more at ease. Taking ownership of all the weirder things I've felt, I tried to make use of it rather than bury my body under the crushing weight of all the casual expectations I've been unable to meet. I tried to have a laugh about it, turning the horror on its head to find the best way to be honest about what I'm going through and then look outward from there. And before I knew it, things felt better. I'd fully harnessed my own method and it helped me grow into the skin that covers my own body.

Going out for dinner with a friend, we were talking about anxiety and graded exposure. I had been trying all kinds of ways of avoiding irrational safety measures that were making me associate situations in my mind with danger, such as hiding my phone in a suitcase. Without me realizing, it had heightened my psychological comparison with a loaded weapon. My friend had experienced some similar patterns, and I'd already snuck one of the sheets of tactics for dealing with anxiety into his rucksack, confessing later that it was me but that I didn't want to be overbearing by handing it to him in person. After replicating a method my therapist used with me on our walk to dinner, I put my hand in my pocket and took out the non-smartphone this friend had gifted me at Christmas. His face lit up. I proceeded to explain that it was turned off and wasn't carrying a SIM card. The extent of exposure to a fully working phone would steadily increase as it became more comfortable for me.

"You'd just done something that was done with you!" my friend beamed. His background with mental health was different, but I knew both of us could become more confident about everything if we pulled through this as a team.

6:9

"I do love a letter," I replied to a friend, as they jokingly suggested that people would have to write to me after uni. I didn't think they realised that my self-mocking humour had a much deeper earnestness. I really did love it when friends wrote to me. There was one occasion when I didn't know that a friend was back in Brighton for a handful of days until she went out of her way to post me a note through the letterbox asking to meet up for a coffee. Our conversations regularly had mental health in the mix. My keenness to address winter's natural tendency for stirring up a seasonal affective disorder led to another bright connection that corresponded with my village. Being offline could be fun. I took it all much further when I decided to get all my friends at uni to write on a flashcard-sized bit of paper to stick in a scrap book. My idea was that if the going gets tough again, then I'd flick through it to remind me that my disconnection would never be the same as what it was in the past. I've not been able to look at my secondary school yearbook and feel any fondness for my part, so now I've made my own out of contributions from everyone important to my recovery. It was a lifetime supply of meaning all inside one cover.

"You look much better since you first arrived here," my doctor said. "Your general wellbeing has improved dramatically. I mean... you're happy." In hindsight, making a narrative out of all the internal things seems like an obvious route out of the no man's land of a largely invisible mental illness, but I was totally unsure about where it would take me when it started. Hearing that statement from a medical professional after half a year of intensive therapy made me feel like I'd experienced a work of miracle. Getting better was far more difficult for me than doing a marathon. No word of a lie.

My memory of everything that had happened before wasn't making me sad or distressed anymore, so there was no longer a panic voice inside me saying things like: *Here we go again.* Hopefully that was laid to rest. A happy moment wasn't triggering me to reflect gravely on the many that were lost before it. I had been stabilised, and I felt the sufficient energy needed to power through the next struggle without a single wobble. My status with personal devices remained the same, but everything else had completely changed in me. The effect on my confidence was immeasurable, but I still thought it was better to wait until I do more about the central practical issue of avoiding my mobile.

"Okay, well you're doing stuff with your friends and you've got support, so we'll leave it for now. I'll see you in three months," my doctor finished. I'd only wished that I could have opened out earlier. My housemate's girlfriend was already shocked to hear a snippet of what I was battling when I basically lived with her.

"You should have told us!" she cried.

"I didn't know how to," I quickly replied. I couldn't connect all the dots, so I presumed that it would get denounced when I was lacking the self-assurance to talk about it like it was a real thing. My defences were up when I didn't understand why the problem had its trajectory in my mind, so I only learnt how to keep it a secret. I suppose talking about what is really going on is easier said than done. You must be in a comfortable space, and the only solace I gave myself was the dream that all my problems would be over with time. I played the waiting game, until there was no more time to play.

Some of the doodles for my scrapbook included phone numbers, as suggested by those concerned with conventional contact, but one person really touched on the social dilemma around connectivity in a way that I'd never expected.

"Thank you for being so inactive on the socials!" it read. I paused to think about this one. It seemed that she was grateful for a connection, but offline. Perhaps she was unhappy about what the socials did to her relations with people. Concentrating on a social life away from the socials was appreciated by people standing in front of me, but a thank you for it was something else entirely. If it meant something profound without any disingenuous compliment coming from a user, then I hoped that it produced enough sentiment for people to enjoy catching up with me when I wasn't carrying an online device. When talking about plans for the next year, my friends came up with the idea of a group of us living together in London. It was agreed that we'd all have to get something lined up to pay the rent in a more expensive city than our current domain. Big plans, and I initially said yes to keeping a crew this close for the next step, but it was wishful thinking. Focusing on my master's, job searching was quite a big task to perform when I couldn't even comfortably connect with an online seminar room. The pressure mounted from such a grandiose plan, and I'd already shared a vision with friends and family about living outside of Brighton, maybe even Britain. But I knew I had to concede that ambition if contact didn't improve. My housemate and I hung out almost every day while being under the same roof. He was so keen to keep up that dynamic. *If I put my money where my mouth is, how would I feel once I'm there?* Bumping into people every day would be a fantasy in one of the biggest megacities on Earth. I ended up telling my friends to rule me out unless something happened otherwise. I didn't want to let them down in the summer of graduation if all of them had their launch pads ready. They had an opportunity wherever there was Wi-Fi; I was a world apart.

There were times when people talking behind my back had a sharper edge when it was happening online. After asking my housemate to muck in a bit more, after I noticed an imbalance in washing-up responsibilities over a long period, he proceeded to message another member of the house to claim that it was always him being asked when he wasn't the only guilty party. But his finger slipped, and he messaged the wrong person. I'd found out about the exchange from the person he tried to add to the equation, after he'd accidentally sent her a message intended for someone else!

"Bro, you can talk to me about it if you feel I'm being unfair," I huffed directly at him. The tip of the prongs burnt me from being out of the loop, scorching my disconnected body when I heard gossip I didn't like, circulated in the place that once upon a time threatened my life. It wasn't all bad however, since there were also group chat interactions that I found simply hilarious.

"Anyone got eyes on Luke?" a friend posted in a large group chat. I guess it was established that whoever was in my company was left to do the networking. People entered speculations about my whereabouts. It was like *Where's Wally?* but with the socials as the available tool for investigating where I could be. My position was asymmetrical – if I didn't have eyes on a friend I needed to talk to, I had to predict where they would be if no one could find out for me on the spot. Knock on their door, spend a day in the computer cluster hoping that they would enter it to study, listen closely to rumours of where they're hanging out. A new job, perhaps? I didn't mind if it took a few days to find them. It was *Where's Wally?* real-life edition. I'd normalised it by now, learning to live within the limits I had, knowing that this was the extent of what I was ready for in this online-led world. But as term went by, and the attendance to my online classes remained the same, knocking on my parents' door always led to Mum trying to persuade me to tell my tutors about everything. I neither told my therapist about this part, nor agreed that this sort of thing was part of the uni's job. Combined with Mum asking about the duration of my treatment, these difficult questions added up to another stressful scenario.

"There isn't a time scale for this, Mum. I haven't entered surgery for an internal organ!" I imagined a doctor cutting back my scalp to reveal the upper half of my bobbly brain, Hannibal Lecter-style. When tending to tissue, a judgement of time frames and a diagnosis are naturally things loved ones ask to address their worries. *What was going on in there?* I did at times want to see a comparison through a scanner between an average human brain and mine. My doctor did, however, give an estimate for how long I'd be on sertraline for, and it gave me a funny feeling in my gut.

"Two years," he said confidently. I shouldn't have been surprised really.

"Keep doing what you're doing," the doctor repeated. My tutors still weren't seeing anyone in person, so my full education was at a stalemate. I remained static without escaping the feeling that I could be letting my family down again after everything. I was reading about the history of ideas while receiving hours of psychiatry, making me think to myself: every abstract idea that has been documented by humanity just makes it seem more delicate. Surely, a mobile compressed to the purest utility could buddy up with the organ I use for making sense of things. It turns out that the simpler things about mental health can never give the whole problem complete transparency.

My therapist made a gesture with his hands representing my mobile in one and me in the other. The second hand was bending around the first to move forwards instead of breaking down the problem head-on. I couldn't see that my mental state had changed enough to turn my phone on and call someone. But then I was still consciously pushing the boundary of what I could do – making calls on my housemates' phones on my own accord seemed to be going well when it got me doing stuff with my mates without any stress. Right, next step: send something in a group chat, that old chestnut that used to be a pillar of my tragic past. I thought I'd never participate in one again, but now I sent a selfie to tell everyone that it was me on a friend's smartphone, giving them an update. Wally did all the work this time. And when my friends were asking me what I wanted to do for my final birthday as a student, I felt prepared to take a far bigger leap. My housemate made a group chat, and all the members were picked by me and only me. A day event to get friends together, put into plan, with attempts to keep up a buzz and a sense of direction. The agency wasn't unwelcome when I felt it every so often. This was the socials. It was where everything in the name was organised by my peers. I proved to be able to work around its association with pain and fear without it becoming unmanageable. I wasn't even bothered when I heard that somehow my old Facebook account had been added to the chat without a single individual there having it as a friend, much to the astonishment of my other friends who didn't even know it existed. My account didn't feel like a part of me anymore, but that didn't change other people's point of view. It was on their mental territory, and my real-life practical position wouldn't change them from thinking that it was a number just like anyone else's.

"You've got an account! Will you accept my friend request?" a couple pleaded.

"Yeah, I've got a Facebook account," I said, with a hint of pride. "I used to be on there as much as you or anyone else." It took time for them to believe it. Meanwhile, I almost couldn't believe that they were showing slight offence that I didn't accept their friend request. Apparently, it's not cool to be aired, even if the person on the other side hasn't been online for half a decade.

"Sorry guys, I promise it's not personal," I laughed. It felt like more of an accomplishment to please my friends if they couldn't connect with me the easy way. They've kept in touch anyway.

6:10

"I actually really liked writing a letter. Can I do it again?" a friend asked shyly.

"Course you can. Never hesitate!" I urged. New and alien to the young adult, I egged on people's enthusiastic comparison of writing letters with a fairy tale or historic period. If they wanted a pen pal, they knew who to ask. There were plenty of pigeons near me too, if the price of stamps was a little steep or one couldn't be bothered to nip to the post office. One friend looked up the price of a carrier pigeon online. We were amused to find that there were results matching the search, although I suspected that if it wasn't a scam then it would probably be breaking the law. I sometimes pretended to be outraged at the suggestion from someone that I didn't have a phone, telling them that the informant was a tell-tale who had deceived everyone to create embarrassment. There was always a smartphone within reach. I made a grab for it, to playfully confuse them, saying that it was mine, before taking a silly selfie with the enquirer. When the phone was unlocked by its owner, the different expressions around the room put me in a fit of giggles.

"Hey! When did you take that picture?" What was far less intentional was putting a friend in shock that I could turn up at any moment in the same place as them.

"How did you know that I was here?!" I'd only listened to the talk stemming from the socials, but there was an assumption that I couldn't have known, because I wasn't connected like everyone else. It was that very peculiar position that made me tune in differently when I wanted to socialise.

"Nah, all jokes aside, I saw you on my snap maps and fancied coming," I said.

"Shut up," my friend laughed. "You couldn't have known which part of the beach we were on." If it was a bigger group, then I knew they would gravitate to a certain spot by the pier. Light detective work. But I did state quite frankly to my mate that one day he'd be on a beach in a completely different part of the world and I'd emerge out of the sea to greet him. Weirder things could happen. In my pursuit of happiness, my mind had become programmed to listen to friends who were organizing the next social event, making sure that I'm in the right place at the right time to convene with the tide of herd-like behaviours. Like Darwin's theory of evolution, but with a young person's valuable social life without a mobile, I felt connected by developing this habit much further.

Things took a bit of a twist when my friend was at a point in between having her phone stolen and her new SIM being activated. As soon as she was out of reach for Wi-Fi, she had no working device on her.

"I'm going to know how you feel now," she mourned. We knew that our friends were on the beach and I joined her for the walk over. I admitted to her that I felt momentarily cut off as if I was journeying solo.

"Well, I'm with you, so I know we'll bump into them," she said optimistically. *We'll see where this goes.* After a few minutes, she vented her frustration at the scenario.

"I don't know how you do it. I don't even know who's going to be there or what," she said. I felt very calm seeing the experience play out in the centre of town for someone else. It would be very strange to go from having a working smartphone to missing it when you're intending to meet up with friends.

"Like, there's a chance we won't even find them, then what do we do?" she continued. In fairness, I had no idea like on other occasions, but seeing as the possibility of being unable to track them was very new to her, I assured her that I wasn't stressed because I'd grown used to being out in public without being connected. This seemed to console her. Ten minutes later, we bumped into her boyfriend who was also making his way to the beach.

"What!? How? This would not happen if you were not here," she exclaimed. I'd deliberately chosen a route that would increase the chances of crossing paths with friends coming from the student area. My eyes watched, and normally I spotted people earlier as I couldn't afford to switch off in public if I wanted to function while my machine was absent from service. I had to learn to do without, because there were also a lot of things I couldn't do.

Mum had been sending emails to tutors in my name, like during the first lockdown, and my huge summer project was closing in so she finally persuaded me to explain why I haven't been attending and that I would like to see someone in person. My tutor offered it in no time. It turned out that seeing a university professor wasn't nerve-wracking after admitting to them that I couldn't do the online classes. This tutor didn't know me like the one who got me to the finish the year before, but from the way Mum was telling it, he seemed informal with his mention of coffee over email. Cool. I had no issue getting to a place at a specific time.

"Good to see you, thank you so much for meeting up with me." It was my first proper interaction with a tutor for the whole term so I made sure to express my gratitude. As soon as we sat in his office, I tried hard to force out any comparisons in my head to sitting opposite my therapist because the distance between me and them was the same in both settings. The tutor was looking at me like I was an anxious wreck, but didn't ask for any explanations.

"I do sympathise . . ." he began, on the topic of the Zoom call, "I find it very difficult when there's a department meeting with over a hundred people on one call – you can't properly discuss anything or hear out what someone wants to add." I tried to move the conversation onto history, a subject I loved and wished I could have learnt more about from in-person guidance after absorbing some great texts without the opportunity to talk to anyone about them. To my relief, the tutor observed that I'd put the hours into reading, although he told me that I had little direction towards the thousands of words that I had to produce for submission. I didn't know what I was looking for in my studies because I hadn't followed the yellow brick road I would have found with contact. I thought hard about a topic that would please him on the spot so that I wouldn't have to contact him again to confirm it. It didn't come. He asked me to email him once I'd read some more stuff with a narrowed down search. After thanking him profusely for letting me sit in front of him for an hour, he then took an oddly different tone as he asked me very gently if I would like to attend a social event for the course after the final project had been submitted.

"Yeah sure," I responded without getting the link. I realised later that he thought that socializing must have been my paralyzing worry rather than the socials between it. *Interesting.* I did hope to see him again to talk about my work but the gap between sending and answering emails was too wide. This was what I was working with now. A few usual faces down, it was to the computer cluster to work on a dead campus over the summer. It became hard to distinguish the difference between motivation and desperation under those conditions. If I didn't pass, then I knew I would be facing a tsunami of depression that would make me feel like a total failure again.

6:11

I thought I could see the home stretch for my entire course as it was all lining up. That was when I tested positive for Covid-19. After a bout of cursing in the bathroom, I called my housemate's name and told him the news. Only one other member of the house got the same result, so I went into quarantine in my bedroom alone. My online-related social non-existence was to become a walled reality, just after I thought I'd overcome it. And I didn't take it well. With no smartphone, every inch of mobility I'd managed to maintain was swept beneath my feet. I couldn't handle this on top of everything else. I was different. I needed the outdoors and people more than anyone. I couldn't contact the world without it. Since starting my treatment ten months before, I'd had no panic attacks, but an especially ferocious one hit me to the point where I was sweaty and shaky. It was hard to tell if it was a sickness or a part of my lifetime malaise that was triggering my eyes and hands to dart around, trying to cling to any course of action that looked safe and secure. *How do I tell work? Where am I going to type for my deadline? My tenancy runs out in less than a week. I'm isolating within my overall isolation, a pitfall after the gradual climb out of the mess.* These outcries raced within my skull. I tried to figure out how I was going to tell my parents so I desperately tried to crawl out of the dark to read out Mum's mobile number through the bedroom door to my housemate. The timing felt like it couldn't have been more inconvenient, my village evaporating, therapy sessions postponed...

There was a knock on my window. It was fortunate that my bedroom was facing out next to the front door of the house. Mum was standing outside with a face mask on, so I copied her, before climbing up onto the large windowsill that had become my communicative lifeline. Ten days was my jail sentence, and the fever was horrendous. Millions of people had gone through this, but I was really annoyed at myself at first, having been so inundated with tasks while I should've known that this would eventually come. There was no time to spare. The Brighton marathon was in less than a month and I was studying, and working, and moving out, and recovering from... everything. Quarantine is objectively tough, but I wasn't coping. I was inferior, and a lot of help was needed for the fresh mental battle that commenced. My parents and housemates brought me food and water. There was even a handwritten quiz posted under my door. It was hard to accept that all the imagery and delusions from the summer before uni were coming back to define the end of the era.

"Can you take this from me please?" I muttered, as I dropped a penknife in a plastic wallet that Mum held open outside the window.

"Do you need me to get help?" she asked. It wasn't psychosis or schizophrenia, but my thoughts were telling me that I should only have awful things happen to me, and that I was foolish to believe that any cloud parting would make the storm less severe.

Everything good that had happened in the last four years was wrongly made insignificant. I couldn't plan out my coursework as my head was in tatters. This infection was such a common situation of the day but I'd embraced my negative dialogue like I did when I was a teen and didn't feel that there was anything around me that would stop me believing it. My shelter, the offline life that I constructed, only needed a suspension to leave me unprotected from everything before it came back with a vengeance. The connected world outside my door moved and weaved around its parts, a fact I couldn't intervene in from my alternative position, so I was therefore defeated.

I looked up and saw my friend post something through my letterbox. Before I could process what was going on, I failed to dart up onto the sill in time to croak her name loudly enough. My body showed its weakness from the sickness during the awkward climb. I knew this friend was moving out of Brighton before my isolation was done. If I didn't see her again, it's on me. This practical hindrance determined that I couldn't compensate for being cut off from the world, quite literally. I shouted for my housemate and asked him to message her on my behalf. I had to try, but time felt long in a way that only reminded me of the dreadful thoughts that were racing the meters between the walls of my bedroom. *I'm going to lose them all again, aren't I? Just like when I was younger. I can't connect with people; I only contradict myself and now it'll feel worse as the quantity of the real emotional costs are going to leave me dead and buried.* I lay my head down on my bed. The trauma inducing familiarity was extraordinarily unsettling to the point where I was afraid to try and sleep when the fever made me shiver in my sweaty cold bath of a mattress, every slight movement a single battle against the growing weakness of my body. *I'm all alone in the end. Death by disconnect.* Now my body seemed to be faring the same as my mind.

I woke up in a cold pool, wondering what was real and what

was a dream. It was still dark outside. I had no device in my room that could tell me the time, so my hallucinations trickled with additional uncertainty. It's usually advisable to breathe when weird things are happening to you. I passed out and dreamt about people enjoying online activity so much, that they decided to quit their offline lives. I was the only one left in a now barren landscape, because I wasn't existing online. Everyone else had moved on, and I was separated and lost. They were upgrading towards infinity and connecting in a way that I couldn't possibly imagine. Everyone was informed, and they could interact with anyone whenever they pleased. *What could they possibly want from me? There was nothing I had that they didn't.* Suddenly, I heard knocking coming from the outside of my isolated world. Someone must be taunting me. Perhaps I looked like an ape in captivity, having visitors knocking on the window of my enclosure, prompting me to react in a way that would entertain a patronizing onlooker. A second wave of knocking came. *What do they want now?* They've already mocked me once to prove their triumph. No, I think someone in the online world genuinely wanted to reach me. Aid was finally arriving well after I felt absolutely humiliated by a superior online race. I woke up and dashed out of my bed to show a sign of life to my mum outside the window. She'd brought me a coffee and a croissant – the calm café sent straight to me.

"Morning, you alright?" she said. I'd forgotten how weak I'd become as I croaked out something resembling a cross between a toad and a man who'd sunk a bottle of whiskey.

"I'm not good," I managed. The voice I'd been handed before, confident and clear, sounded brittle to the point of snapping. All the support I'd received felt like it had reached a zero-sum result. I later tried to knock loudly on the ceiling of my room to show solidarity with my other housemate in the thick of their own isolation. We exchanged letters on each of our turns for the bathroom respectively. Unfortunately, neither of us could understand morse code but I was informed that a lot of our friends had also tested positive at similar times. A quick chat with my housemate through the window offered a break from the assault on my mind, but it was only piecemeal, however. I sat during the evening feebly strumming my guitar, and I got bored without the prospect of YouTube tutorials to learn songs. People could access these whenever they please. *What was the point? I can't do what anyone else can. I'm the worst.*

My negative self-talk continued its barrages against all the things that had got me to where I was in life. I should have been grateful here like no other time before. I wanted my family and friends to see me get better, so I can give more to them for the heroism they've shown me without any obligation or rational incentive. If you struggle to word what love is then think about where you put it, the greatest passion to come out and make us want to carry on. It's dished out in whatever way our personalities grant the most effective according to what we devote our efforts to. I wanted to live, so that I could use the things I've learnt about the darkest of places to help other people never linger there for too long. There was a knock on my window so I composed myself. My curtains weren't drawn and my light was on so that any dark silhouette out in the evening could easily have seen me. One of my friends from next door was standing outside my window, and she introduced me to her little sister.

"I really wanted her to meet you so we've stopped by on the way to the pub, if you don't mind," she said.

I laughed, "That's okay, I haven't got any plans this evening." My voice had returned like it had never been gone.

"Aww, well I know you'd be there if you weren't in quarantine," my neighbour said. I couldn't let my sickness destroy me. Being alone all the time was the biggest misconception I could ever have. The good news was that I could use my abundance of spare time to stick entries from all my friends in my scrap book. The infamous 'brain fog' may have threatened my memory, but the connections I had with the people who'd help me rediscover life itself were right in front of me, recorded on paper. Now was the perfect time to use them.

It was the first time I'd ever phoned in sick for work. Mum sent a text on my phone with my positive PCR result attached. The uni would give an extension to my deadline in due consideration. The rest of my house were saying that they were very bored due to half their mates being in quarantine. I was glad to hear that our tenancy was extended. I'd even been asked to move into my friends' house with them while they were also isolating and I took it up in the blink of an eye. We had little to say, but we had each other – mental health first aid on a plate. My perception before was the most skewed it could be, and I learnt that disruption does not mean that it's the end of the world, a fact I struggled to remain secure about in the heat and cold of feverish dreams.

Part VII

7:1

I didn't want to move back to my parents' house, because my social body's spine relied on living with friends. When I shared the dread of moving out of student accommodation forever, my neighbours offered a helping hand. A spare room for three weeks; the perfect base until I figured out the next step in my offline life. I was bidding farewell to friends moving away from Brighton with the certainty that against all the odds, they would see me again. Canada, Spain, Saudi Arabia – who cared how far away they'd be? I didn't know how I was going to do it, but I insisted that there'd be a way. It took some time for it to sink in what the changes for immediate contact would do as people were leaving my village in Brighton indefinitely. There wasn't yet time to dwell on the insecurity it could cause, however. I was finishing my dissertation and resuming running. Someone told me that Covid-19 would attack parts of your system that you could call a weak point. For many, this would apparently be the lungs, but my soft underbelly was unsurprisingly psychological and it would take longer than the ten-day isolation period for the brain fog to clear enough for me to read and write like before. I went into my school office to ask for the extension to my deadline, and the receptionist assured me that I would certainly receive it, despite the inevitable difficulty in showing evidence via a form. I hoped that my application was sufficient because I wasn't going to be checking my email to see if it was confirmed. I typed away with the uncertainty hovering over me, aware that anyone would check on their smartphone instantly if they have received an extension from the examination office. Coming back to my temporary residence in the evening, I was taken off guard when my housemate's boyfriend put it bluntly when it was relayed in front of me what had been shared about my phoneless life.

"Yeah, you're fucked," he added, before turning around in the kitchen to cook. That comment couldn't have come at a worse time, considering I was preparing to harbour more responsibilities for life after uni.

"Oh, by the way ..." my temporary housemate began as she handed her phone to me. My new housemates were bemused at the unexpected role of being my social media, but a new challenge arose while my brain was still fogging up to the point that I felt as daft as a brush. Dad believed I was still with my friends where I was isolating, having dropped a care package containing my medication to them soon before they were moving out of Brighton. The day I ran out of sertraline, I began to panic as I couldn't figure out where my supplies were. I had to message people, work out where the package had gone, find out where anyone who could be potentially holding it was currently staying. *Were they even in Brighton?* Maybe the bag was thrown away given that the contents were unknown to anyone taking it. After sitting in the lounge of my current accommodation, trying to keep it together in front of my housemates around me, I worked out where it may have ended up. I borrowed a smartphone and made an online call. No answer. I swore loudly. *Okay, think.* I could have knocked on a door, but I remained uncertain of where people were – I wasn't the only individual staying with friends whose tenancies remained running. Then I remembered that one of my housemates in front of me used to be in a swim club with the person my old housemate was staying with. The connection was distant and random, but the socials didn't remove people off friends lists on their own. They encourage people to remain connected to maintain their best strengths. I made a call on Snapchat, of all the platforms, and my friend answered it telling me that the person I believed to be holding my meds was with them.

"I thought it would be you" she said, as she passed her phone over.

"That package, mate: do you have it with you?" I asked my old housemate urgently. "It's got something really important in it. Can you bring it over?" Another close call averted. How long could I keep this up for? It's not always clear in advance that everything is on its way, whether it's medication, or an extension to a deadline. I haven't got long until I break away from living with friends.

There was little time to process the finish line of my course because now I was preparing for a different one that I believed before was impossible to pursue without the conventional contact machine. I had two friends who had also applied to do the marathon with me, one of them having been beside me for our unofficial one. Unfortunately, they now lived outside of Brighton, so I trained alone having no idea what their progress was and how I was going to see them at the starting line. Two weeks to go, and I was feeling the pressure when Mum was telling me that we needed to create a fundraising page. The logistics took a little while to work out.

"And you need to contact your friends, Luke, so you can check which bracket of finish time predictions they're in." There were different start times in half-hour brackets that were colour coordinated according to your estimated finish time. This technicality made planning difficult as I hadn't been in contact with my mates for weeks. I wanted nothing more than to start with one of them beside me, otherwise I'd invent a negative meaning to starting the event solo. I soon became very disappointed. Both friends had bailed and I thought I was beginning the marathon alone.

My family had set up a JustGiving page for people to make donations that would go straight to MIND, instilling a much healthier mindset that was telling me that I was doing this because of my illness, so any issues over connection wouldn't trip me over while I was preparing to do the event. JustGiving involves sending a link out to people to access an individual page. The socials had been turned around in yet another highly controlled way. It was the tool employed for gaining support in a pursuit that was underway after all the destruction between me and my online entanglements. I needed help from their powers, despite all the history. I wrote down my page's link on paper and kept it in my wallet for people to photograph on their phones in passing. My family also sent the link to their friends who'd known me at different stages in my life. A close friend's smartphone was borrowed to send the link in the group chats, my birthday chat being the first. It felt like a huge statement considering the backwardness of my online support system during my teens. The donations came in, and the significant generosity from people I'd spent hours talking to about mental health made me smile. All the substance was brought to the surface for us to accept any vulnerability during the age of socials. I had learnt to live beside it, accepting that it is there and it doesn't always have to tempt people to their detriment. We were online, although no one could buzz a block in my pocket. Unfortunately, I didn't check the weather forecast before doing the longest training run before the marathon. With ten miles to go on a very humid evening, the heavens opened after dusk so I was brawling through soaking wet feet and clothes that seemed to add a few kilograms to my cargo from the sky's downpour. In more rural parts, my best source of light came from the lightning so that my vision could clock the deeper puddles. I couldn't stop though, or it'll get very cold in my light gear. The absence of a portable toolkit only gave me extra wind to reach home.

7:2

"You seemed to have this habit of just turning up at the right time." It almost sounded like I was getting a telling-off.

"Oh hello!" another answered the door. "We were literally just talking about you and wondering how we're going to keep in contact with you, now you've moved out of yours." I walked into their kitchen announcing that whenever someone says my name, I'm going to appear at their front door. I honestly think that because my friends couldn't answer a query by messaging me instantly, the wonder sticks and gets answered when I find them. They were so used to gathering info from their devices that to find me without them at an unexpected time was the work of a magician who was yet to reveal their tricks. The reality was that I'd not always been successful in trying to find my friends on many occasions. Having been told where to meet on the beach one time, it took me about 45 minutes until I found them on a completely different spot. The weather was hot and I didn't need the extra work when I was running the marathon in three days, but I couldn't wave my finger. How could they understand? I couldn't afford to fall out with people because of my disappointment, but this kind of experience would help me remember whom I could trust with certain things in the future. They wouldn't tell me about upcoming social events if I was upset with them. I do better by being kept out of the dark. It's all about communication after all, and I had to agree with my doctor when he said that I was bound to miss out on things.

I'd heard this name before, and it wasn't a common one.

"She's from Brighton, she went to school here," my friend said. She hadn't asked which school but I had a hunch. The new member of a house I was hanging out with a lot had moved in, and it meant that someone from my old world could be coming in very close proximity to my new. I had to remind myself why my apprehension was reminding me of being small. When hosting a birthday party, I arrived and eventually saw her: an old classmate walking past me in her own house which she now shared with my friends. I didn't react but it was tough to shake off the anxiety over the collision of old and new: a world where I was inadequate and a world disconnected from anything to do with the former. This was the closest it could get. There's bumping into old school friends in the street and then there's knowing that I was going to be seeing this individual for times to come. It increased the pace of my mind as I was reminded of how it felt to depart from an unsuccessful social life to a reconstruction. I turned to my close friend beside me and described my hesitation. I tried to remember some of the methods for tearing down my barriers put up by anxiety. *Now was the time. No more thinking.* I strolled up to towards this old face and introduced myself. She looked gobsmacked and claimed that she hadn't recognised me. This was believable, considering I had rejected almost everything about myself from when I was online. It was always going to naturally trickle down to a complete change of appearance in the space of five years. As I was talking to her about school, I found it odd to hear names I hadn't heard in a long time, but it was probably the gentlest collision I could ask for. We quickly became friends. One more troubling boundary breached, and very well timed as it wasn't long until I was making a big public appearance in the city where it all began.

To show good will when I couldn't connect like they could, I wanted to send a parcel containing my friend's favourite shirt after he moved back to Canada. He refused point blank to take part in my preference for letters, but luckily his old housemate and compatriot gave me his own postal address, so I then took up the opportunity. I wrote a letter to my new pen pal across the Atlantic and added the shirt to send from a post office because it felt right. And as I turned to leave, someone with a face mask on greeted me whom I hadn't recognised until she revealed herself to be a friend whom I hadn't seen for months. If I hadn't gone into the post office to perform the deed, the catch up and farewell would never have ensued. I'm grateful for these kinds of reasons to get out and about and potentially bump into people in my village. It turned out she was moving out of Brighton in two days so we arranged to meet up for dinner. It was quite amusing to watch someone write down their phone number for me outside in the street. I presumed that it was a first for them, but I was gathering phone numbers to either keep in my wallet or in a phone book I received as a gift when I was ten. The book allowed me to dial numbers on other people's mobiles if I wanted to get through to them. Who would have thought it would come into good use thirteen years later? I borrowed my sister's phone to make the call the day after.

"Hello?"

"Hello, this is Jason Bourne here. Just kidding, it's Luke. How are you doing?"

"Good, I was literally just thinking about you, and wondering how I'd get in contact."

"This is a secure line, but only for a couple of minutes. Dinner at seven?" Done. If I wanted to reach people on a whim, I'd upgraded my capability without feeling like I'm going to go mad. My therapist asked out of curiosity how I saw my friends, and could see how important it was to address the obstructions to communication. It kept me running, but sustainability was another question when more of my friends were leaving outbound. Using is different from possessing. A step in the right direction isn't a destination. My general improvement had also led me to try and start dating without my phone, with letters being exchanged regarding a time to meet somewhere. It showed commitment, granted. There was one occasion when someone had to cancel when they had to work overtime for a wedding reception. She later explained her panic at being unable to notify the sharp turn, and explained that she messaged a mutual friend who carried it on to my housemate, who then in turn fed it to my friend who was out for a coffee with me. When I later discovered the trail of this chain of communication, I was in awe of the support network that existed. The fundamental issue continued, but I was feeling so good about the year that I called off therapy, leaving only the occasional visit to my doctor. It was safe to say that I was feeling fine, and it looked like the best was yet to come.

7:3

I wasn't sure where to begin. Funds had been raised for MIND but the timings and equipment procedure were still unclear. Keeping still on the day before the marathon proved to be difficult despite my friend's humorous reminder of the circumstances. I wasn't nervous yet, but characteristically around anxiety, a lack of nerves before something big can make you worry about there not being any worries at all when you question why you're not feeling them. How do connected people prepare for a marathon? I walked down to the base around the finish line to pick up a pack and drop off some things for me to receive after I complete the course. Most of the time I was looking over my shoulders at the other participants. Mum had phoned the local taxi service the day before to book a cab to drop me off at the start line when I needed convenience more than ever. It was peculiar, getting updates from friends on who had donated on my page, but I was thrilled with the contributions, and people told me that they would be beside the track cheering me on. A detached soul would never have expected that in a million years.

The nerves reminded me of departing to Italy, but were now in a much more filtered intensity. The cab Mum had booked was running late. She phoned them up to enquire about its progress; I simply wanted to walk the two miles towards the start line. None of this surprised me, being all too easy to place the scenario into a prophecy about rough tracks and adversity in the disconnected life I had. Mum said to wait for another ten minutes, but my calm was tested. We eventually walked, and I was somewhat glad that my feet were on the ground where I'd be performing a trial of absolute endurance. Following fellow runners with blue on their backs, I waved goodbye to Mum and established a pace on the tracks. Noticing the AirPods around me, I wondered how many people were running with a smartphone in their possession, but then I remembered that there are watches with similar features.

I ran because of my mind's experiences, and I was feeling like a spearhead thrusting into the blockade that had been resisting and determining everything for me for almost a decade.

The slogan for the event, printed on my top, read, 'The comeback is greater than the setback'. I tried to look past the corniness to imagine myself putting these words into action. This was a day to celebrate coming out stronger than any time before when I was fine. I also saw ahead of me an advertisement for an app for the event, informing the dates for the next Brighton marathon and that runners could sign up for it, as they're undergoing one. The occasional loudspeaker and individual cheer were wonderful. Every bit of help goes a long way, which was why I called the names of friendly faces on route and waved to them if they didn't see me. Greeting someone had always been a turbo boost in any walk of life, and that psychological vitality didn't change now. My pace was careful and never got carried away. I was running through the city where I'd always lived, but only relatively recently opened myself up to in a way that made me happy.

Young people on the side of the road were holding up cardboard signs reading, *'Tap for a power boost'*. I'd make sure to tap any one of them within my reach, feeling the power handed to me as I made contact with these people's brilliance. It was going well, although the wall was as bad as its notoriety suggested. My legs were far denser than flesh and bone, while my tank was only filled with citrus fruits and electrolytes handed to me by volunteers. The sides were quiet by mile eighteen, as the track had brought us between Shoreham power station and the sea, far from the support that was provided in the residential areas of Hove. A bigger presence by now came from paramedics tending to fallen runners in trouble from the sun and strain. I looked away from all of them, hoping that each mile mark wasn't too far away while I held onto any invincible moment that crossed my memory. Looping around to return to the city, every clap and cheer from a spectator was an oasis of the humanity I'd reintroduced myself to. All the laughs and good times with my friends came into the front of my mind, fuelling my feet to fight in the place where I was once brought down to my knees in pain after violent dissociation. People were waiting for me at the finish line. They were waiting to see me come back from every difficulty flying into my face all in one day. The city was organised online, but I'd lived through that reality, tapping for that next power up and setting my eyes towards the finish, triumphant within a square kilometre of where I almost died. Three miles to go ... I told myself that if I started walking, I wouldn't get running again. Above the weight of my legs, I could feel momentum like never before. Two miles to go ... the streets were getting busy with excitement. There was great community spirit out here. People were supporting strangers, letting them know that a challenge so pure and life-affirming earns a friendly interaction for its own sake. I was one of them, offline, but right here reaching the last mile and getting told "Well done!" without having to show any existence in the virtual realm. *Why did it take doing a marathon for me to feel like that? Where was this inclusive attitude when I was on the brink? Many of these people probably measure success in online terms, a measurement that carried me to a place where I collapsed.* Suddenly, I became angry. One mile to go... my head was looking up, putting all the faces on the side of the road out of focus. Both my legs were frenetically pulling everything out of the bag to sprint past everyone. My anger became the remaining fuel.

400 meters to go, I had a snarl on my face in front of the crowds. *They are the online world, and I'm here, tearing this mentality apart.* Full speed ahead. I pushed through everything that was once too much for me on my own. Every little comment that had belittled my path to survival before had made it even more challenging to motivate myself to do anything with my life before this very day. *Now look at me!* The finish line. The burning passion that got me to the end had dissipated. My legs turned to jelly as I slowed to a walk and processed the mental battle that fired up under the threat of exhaustion. I felt that way because of my experience, but that experience will never make me hate everyone who uses the thing I'd damaged myself with. I asked a fellow runner what the time was. He could barely respond but showed me his smartwatch, marking my successful settlement with the digital divide: cautious, but amicable.

One of the first things my family and friends did as I joined them was take photos of me for the socials. Apparently, my race number had also been attached with a tracker that people could follow on a site by typing in my race number. My family got my finish time without even needing to see me, and for the rest of the day there were messages sent to me from my friends. With much of my support deriving from sources I didn't possess for myself, it felt strange to be at the centre of attention, so it was great to hear that a friendly face had also done the marathon, little to my knowledge until after we finished. We united through a mate's phone and congratulated each other. I was grateful for the in-person gesture, and glad that my running face wasn't caught on camera by my friends. Brighton was the place where I'd been at the bottom. Now during that moment, there was nothing negative on top of me.

7:4

People who'd recently come out of uni were referring to the transition to 'the real world out there'. I had the garden centre as my security net, but my attempts at keeping up a wave of activity at the tail end of the summer began to become feebler. I applied for a seaside bar job where the manager only asked for my name and phone number. The next day, I kept my smartphone switched on and in my pocket, although I didn't know if that was enough to notice the call if it came. It was on vibrate only, so my left hand remained clasped around it, as I went for a walk around town with my friend to kill some time. It didn't make things easier. Did I want to do bar work? Another friend had been working there for a few months so I had help if things got tricky.

I turned to my friend on the high street. "I've got my phone in my pocket. Can you call it?" After a look of surprise, she complied with the simple request. I felt my phone to see how noticeable it was, like squeezing a trigger with the safety catch on. My focus sharply changed... hang on.

"Would you be up for going there?" I asked as my friend half-jokingly expressed her glee at holding the number of the 'one without the phone'. A different manager at the bar told me he'd almost forgotten to call, and then gave me a trial shift on the spot. I'd managed to get another job.

"Contact my secretary," I told my old housemate, when he asked how he'd reach me to finalise a plan. My friend, and now co-worker, had also mentioned that the bar rota came through a group chat so she texted my hours to the phone that Mum relayed messages from. It was a delicate chain of info but I went along with it. The sun was out and I was tired of working extra shifts at the garden centre. The stress of adapting to big changes made me grow irritable about communication breakdowns and feeling separated from my old information sources. The differences in my needs were really starting to show, as I was struggling to admit to myself that it was possible I required a babysitter. Support networks can change, but an old connection can't always guarantee that they're going to be there for you on demand. I slumped after feeling 100% certain only days before that I'd buried my despair forever. How was this possible?

My family acted as scribes, reading messages sent to me by a small number of people who otherwise would have been impossible to contact if they weren't regularly interacting with people I could knock on doors to see. I would tell my sister to write down messages to maintain contact with people while trying to contain the issue. Nevertheless, the expectations led to a scenario that felt uncomfortably out of my control. Straightforward texts became transmitted into gossip far and wide. People I trusted handed my number around, and I was swept along by an avalanche of messages from people acting in their ordinary fashion from the common smartphone. I wasn't ready, and I felt a landslide of worry and stress over how my friendships and focus would fare from handling the casual exchanges that brought back my nightmare in the house where it all originated. After all my work to get better, the fear of regression caused me to pace my room with my hands in my hair at the thought that I'd travelled back in time to the wreckage of dreams about the end to my disorder. It was worse when I struggled to communicate it to friends.

"Well, it's not that bad if people want to reach you" one of them scoffed. It was that bad. The tangibility of my issue had its framework of spoken truths crumpled into an unconvincing tale that related to no one left in my village. I took Murphy's Law as the largest truth where all hope was vacating out of my core again. The light at the end of the tunnel is the head lamp of an oncoming train. And it was a bullet.

"We need to find you some kind of support worker, Luke, because you can't carry on like this," Mum said. I explained to my doctor about my unsuccessful moves, telling him that my smartphone was off and my secretaries had stood down.

"Do you want to use a phone?" he said directly. I decided that because my answer wasn't yes or no once again, I should resume therapy. I entered the consultation feeling foolish for calling it off a month previously. I grew sour as I became stuck again. Everyone could message each other at will and organise the next meeting, while I was tense by the time I was in their company, heavily anxious that it was all going to slip away. My family asked where I was heading with my life with the prescient idea that I should know by now, given that they'd spent a fortune on my treatment without the issue of contact showing any change on the surface. Once I'd moved back home to experience my student habits clashing with Mum's 'don'ts', it was already getting heated at home, and the arguments with my parents combined the unsettling scenario with the disappointment at the recurrent outcome of carrying no device.

"Ultimately, you've achieved nothing!" That part made me lose it, and a series of domestic fallouts led to threats that I'd be kicked out of the house. There definitely wouldn't be any coming back if I was sleeping rough with my illness. My foreshadowed escape had only quadrupled the force of my break, as I landed myself back in the captivity of a dislocated mind.

After a few days of wobbling, I found some space to move. Two friends of mine were running the London marathon that autumn, after they both had to stop half-way in the unofficial one we did together earlier in the year. There was some unfinished business, and I wanted to be there to see them seal the deal after being dispirited after my failed attempts to organise trips with friends. Setting off from Brighton alone wouldn't put me off from trying to find them, but my desperation to get away from home made me rush, and I failed to arrange an accurate meet-up point in an event that attracted numbers of people parallel to a population of a country. We'd only texted to say roughly where we would find each other around the area, but Trafalgar Square in London was less than vague. Rising from the London Underground station, I already sensed that I'd given myself the hardest task of all the times I'd magically appeared in a friend's location. Dodging past pedestrians down the path to the finishers area, I broke into a run through the giant metropolis, containing masses of people whom I couldn't narrow down to my friends. *Not a chance, surely*. It looked like I'd messed up this time. *Was there a payphone anywhere?* I'd recently tried to use one in Brighton, but to no avail. *How would I know when they'd finished? Should I wait?* Perhaps they'd registered the situation and conceded the plan. I turned back from the stone archway at the edge of the square and gave up. *What a waste of a trip.*

"Luke!" a familiar voice bellowed. No way. I rushed up to my mate with his finisher's medal on, and threw my arms around him, without considering whether his joints could take it. My day started from there; the last stage of *Where's Wally?* completed to add to the celebrations. A friend of theirs I'd never met before had tried my phone in the middle of the race.

"I spoke to your mum before I'd even met you!" she laughed. It was a total fluke and the joy that it gave led me to agree to visit our friend living in Edinburgh, the achievement of our union as memorable as the good times that followed it. How could I refuse when my personal growth felt so suffocated at home. It persuaded me to make the initial contact by phone amidst all the stress, so with minimum information of what we had in store for each other, I travelled for the day by rail to the Scottish capital to find my friends at Waverley station. All I gathered was that we were looking to climb to the tallest point in the British Isles, Ben Nevis. My three friends tactically covered every entrance of the station, and they were relieved to find me and see that I'd packed the right gear for mountaineering. My doctor told me that the thought of my friendships withering away due to a lack of contact was invalid when people were accustomed to it, but my irrationality in an isolated state dominated me in a house I connected with psychological horror.

I came back from my break and immediately wished I stayed in Scotland. I wanted to stay with my mate and never come back. *Who knows when I'll see him again. Maybe never.* That's the way it appeared to be going. The parasite in my brain was fully awake now, noshing away at any human association I'd gathered so that I wasn't the same as I was at uni. *My friends might not like me anymore.* I was narrating awful things in my head when people were out of my earshot, and re-entry became as nerve-wracking as coming back to Earth from space. As I should've known, the bar job was a bad idea. I'd been denied any hours while the boss didn't bother wiping my name of the rota on the group chat. Finding out at the pub when my self-esteem had already hit an iceberg, I had sunk into the sea of doubts with my hands tied up.

7:5

Look online. There are so many websites where you can find opportunities. Inertia. Motionlessness. Pain. I mourned to Mum that I'd rather be amputated than be here now. When Grandma suggested that I should go to a hypnotist to pull out the roots of my issue, I felt like I was willing to try anything. It would give me something to do, anyway. She searched online for practitioners based in Brighton, and I deliberately selected one who gave a street address. More mysterious knocking abounded, as I pressed the doorbell to an apartment building at 11:30 am on an overcast November's day.

I heard movement approaching from inside and a senior women opened the door, "Hello?"

"Hi there, is this the hypnotherapy practice?"

"Yes!"

"Would it be possible to book an appointment here?"

"Why yes! Please come in." I edged after her into her home and was asked to explain everything.

"I've never had someone knock on my door before, but I suppose that makes perfect sense for you, so well done for doing it." Her voice was soothing, and I could feel her eyes reading me which had an effect of great calmness.

"I can tell that you're very stuck, but you've got the will to get yourself unstuck. Now, I can't promise you that my work will make you unstuck, but I can promise that some of the things that we'll be doing will live with you forever," she stated clearly. It sounded good and I was willing to learn; willing to try everything that would improve my capacity to cope with the situation that defined my life.

"It dominates the world. I get fed up with it too. I much prefer talking with people face to face than on a screen," she

217

commented. We set a time and date for me to return for a session and she asked me what hour of what day I was brightest. I simply wanted to crack on as soon as possible. That would make everything brighter.

"And if you can't make it, or we need to rearrange, is there a way of contacting you?" There isn't anything that would have made me miss this but I gave her my email, seeing as that seemed to be satisfactory. I wasn't going to check it, so if she was unable to give the session when we planned, I'd just have to find out at the door then hadn't I?

Another step into the unknown. The hypnotherapist told me that she normally recorded herself reading out a transcript from the first session, along with methods she'd use to try and re-tune my brain. I could tell she'd never come across my issue in her work before, as she had to adapt the transcript to a handwritten document that I could read without any electronic device.

"You'll have to excuse my poor handwriting. I rarely write at all." I didn't question her credentials, but it took me a little while to get used to receiving treatment in her lounge, a private space filled with personal belongings that became the environment around the exposure of my thought patterns. I explained what treatment had happened following my diagnosis and assured her that it helped, but didn't quite feel complete. The appointment opened with a simple theory that the hypnotherapists' practice derived from. Two halves to the mind: The thinker and the prover.

"What the thinker thinks, the prover proves," – this was the basis for delving into the subconscious. Treating the phone like a hazardous object hereby makes it hazardous, a manifestation we were trying to break. If I changed what I thought, my prover mind would stop latching onto a particular idea which confirmed the worst. Bingo. Before I knew it, I was slipping into a hypnotic state, and then I was gently told to close my eyes.

"Your unconscious mind is there to protect you, but sometimes it gets it wrong." I could have listened to her voice for hours. It was the only sound I could hear, but soon I had to clear my throat to put my shift in.

"It gets sensitive to some things that aren't important and won't pose a threat at all if you adapt your thoughts to them." I'd never heard my relationship with the online world put like that before. The thing with me was that I had my guard up because everyone was online, and with the length of time I'd spent running away from it, no one ever got let in. My unconscious mind branded it a threat, and now this hypnotherapist had given me direct orders to lower the drawbridge, and let her change my mind's conception of communication technology as a dangerous thing while we live in a time where it's almost surgically attached to human life. I wasn't fighting now, and I felt relaxed. My suit of armour melted away, making me feel like a feather. Then some questions filtered into my subconscious, and I began to speak in my state.

"I want to tell the difference between information that's important and not so..." *information that I can put a value on while recognizing how healthy my networking behaviour really is when it comes to benefits being received more consistently, with the negative side received when I've gone too far in trying to uncover what's happening in everyone else's life to the point where I don't feel secure inside my own body. I lost my sense of self without satisfying the compulsion to follow this destructive route to discontentment from an overload of invented necessities. If I could bring my mind and body closer together, then I'll know what's truly important to me while being able to co-exist and further feel safer about what's outside myself.* This was at the deepest root. I'd learnt something completely new about myself.

We arranged a time for me to collect my transcript, and she instructed me to read it to myself every day, with instrumental music in the background. I found my own words held within and felt myself slowly swinging to a different thought pattern. Like with my meds, anything I initially didn't take too seriously about the practice was amended. I had been educated once more about cognitive behaviour so I agreed with the hypnotherapist that yes indeed, this work was going to live with me for the rest of my life. I followed her recommendation to book a second appointment at minimum and kept up with one more piece of homework she'd given me. I was writing down three good things that happened to me every day. A lot of the entries mentioned friendly faces bumping into me for a spritely chat. A very special case was when my friend, who had moved away to Barcelona, returned for a visit and asked my former housemate for my home address before knocking on the door. I wasn't in but she had passed a note on to Mum telling me where I could find her in the city. This simple act absolutely blew me away. How could I doubt the security of our friendship? This was incredible and it made me want to go out with her and share good times just as we had before.

7:6

"What do you want to achieve by the end of this session?"

Inside my mind: *No idea. Well, no. Many ideas, but some faith in their conversion would be nice. What is my purpose here? What motivates me? Go.*

Outside my mind: "To break down any further barriers between my mind and body, so I can be more confident in asserting how I feel." That seemed to suffice. The hypnotherapist then proceeded as if I'd given a correct password.

"The solution is inside of you. It's about bringing it out, not searching for something you don't have." *If there was a spirit in there, could it please fly out to my mate I haven't seen for years and send him a text message?* No, that wouldn't help me sleep better at night. The hypnotherapist was trying to help me understand the track where my issue worsened itself when I started using the socials. I was also happy that she had a sense of humour.

"You know the other week, I was out for a walk and this person was coming straight towards me, eyes down on their phone, until I shouted 'Boo!' and made them leap aside." This got me laughing a lot. Anyone telling me stories like that was some of the best medicine out there. It brought the issue from my mind to the outside world. Mobile data did bring some adverse effects.

"We're going to perform an exercise called timeline. I'm going to ask you to think of a memory from before this crisis began to brew, to track how it may have led towards your unhealthy online behaviour."

"Okay," I was determined. Memories played out once I'd focused on past occasions that came to the fore that the hypnotherapist instructed me to pluck out. Her questions pulled them out of the deep only minutes after I closed my eyes. The childhood memories down the line were totally random, nothing at all which I expected to have any relevance with my experience of the socials, but they represented the build-up of the feeling of missing something, and furthermore always being a few steps behind the people whom I called my friends. I felt excluded when a moment played out to trigger this, and I was recalling a recurring sequence of this back as far as when I was only five years old. Every time an incident came out of my subconscious memory, the hypnotherapist asked if the consequences were due to a fault of my own or other people. When I put the blame on myself, she asked me to go further back in time to a point when a comparative feeling was also there, stretching back to an occasion in my infancy that stretched the limits of my living memory. I finally changed my answer for this one, an early case of a mean joke played by a group in pre-school, where a game traditionally involving a chase around the playground had been turned into a trick where the other participants all ran away from me as a team.

I had no knowledge that they'd changed the game to pit it against me. The conclusion of this exercise was that this feeling kept coming back, throughout my childhood, and took a deadly twist when I began using the socials with this predisposition. My introduction to the online world in my teens was tainted by this sequence from my childhood, a regular insecurity that stuck out and affected my self-esteem throughout my life. The daily situations with my peer group dotted it all together. A world apart in my eyes, and a contemplation that the inferiority complex that came with it was a timeless truth that pointed everything about my suffering to be a fault of my own. Not true. I opened my eyes and understood that it wasn't all on me, and whenever the pain came back, I was wrong to tell myself that I felt this way because of my own behaviour alone. I was also unlucky with how my mind reacted to my use of the socials. At the time, a lot of the activity on there was never going to do much good for my mood. I should have waited but the social pressure was simply too heavy for my vulnerable thirteen-year-old self.

"No, I'm living without it because I'm not ready for it," was what a mature version of me would have declared. Instead, my life was transformed by something I couldn't control.

"If you need anything, you can always contact me," the hypnotherapist said, as I stood up ready to leave. My head felt lighter, my feet springier.

"Thank you, goodbye," I said. I didn't think that I could always contact her, but I knew that her sessions had helped. We'd drawn up an accurate map of what all of this was influenced by. I should be comfortable saying no when someone tries to bring me into their mental life that's fabricated by the socials. They can never understand my situation there and then, so their behaviour towards me when I'm not connecting with them in their way, is not due to my failings or because they're trying to attack me. They simply want people to stay connected, and the most obvious path of that in the age of the socials is not something I should be stacking against my mental health. If someone's frustrated that I'm not connected, they'd simply have to get over it.

7:7

Getting back to my friend who'd come from Barcelona to Brighton was tricky, but after a miscalculated search and wait at the bar she mentioned, my Catalan comrade finally turned up, and I avoided feeling like a muppet by sitting at another table with some friends who I'd bumped into at a fortunate time. I almost didn't know what to say to her. She'd literally flown in that day; arrived in Brighton, dropped off her baggage where she was staying, and knocked at my parents' house like it was normal. She shrugged when I told her it had turned a shoddy day around. I guessed it wasn't too difficult, seeing as her attitude put it into motion, no mental barriers towards doing it differently out of circumstance and for a good reason.

"She did really well," my former housemate later remarked. To me, it felt like Trafalgar Square. Sometimes I got lucky, and that made the rest of the meet-up have a tint of gold.

I'd got a new job at a vintage clothes store, when Mum told me that I'd received a text from the manager of a small local chain. I didn't hesitate to say 'yes' as soon as I heard from her. The rut was broken, and I was employed in a new environment; a friendly one where I'd even made the cut for the staff Christmas party after only working there for a week. It signalled that I'd entered a new circle of people who could mark my exit from the student routine. Many of them were ex-students and young people, so it was a confident start. The stores also had outdoor clothing rails and I appreciated the watch duty in the busy street as it gave me the opportunity to see friendly faces pass by and rejuvenate my recently stagnated village after the emigration of many uni mates. It couldn't be overstated how key this was in changing my relationship with the city where I rose from the ashes of disintegration before reaching my offline settlement. My excitement with the job was challenged when my greenness faded however, as the warm welcome from some youth-minded characters began to disapprove of one way in which I was doing it all differently from the conventions of mainstream society in an apparently indie store. I had to make Instagram posts for them, featuring me, made by me, and on a very frequent basis.

"It's your turn to make a reel today, Luke." *What's a reel? I thought a reel was a part of a traditional camera.* The company got its staff to create posts on their smartphones. Stress. At first, I managed to avoid the responsibility, but then on a quiet day in the shop, I was up. I'd already told the duty manager that I had no personal account to tag, but this wasn't my friends at uni. This was work, and I couldn't disobey within the four-person team. I was too new, although I did on a couple of occasions politely inform the manager that I hadn't used Instagram for five years. Evidently it had all changed since. It's not a hammer or a screwdriver. How many people saw their posts? There was editing and timings to perform – authorship that, after picking clothes to include in the post, filled me with no idea on how to present. Apparently, the most likes were gained when staff appeared on shot. Fine, I'll wear your stuff and feature my face online, I can do that. Better than me using it. I tried my best to see the funny side of me pretending to be an influencer.

I was more than prepared for a till system, but the iPad supporting it and the encouragement of all staff to pick music behind it left me apprehensive. I had to keep thinking to myself that this was work. Seeing as my DJing of songs was mostly limited to my record collection, the temptation to play other songs at work got me, and happily both co-workers and customers responded well. This was only the beginning though. On a couple of occasions, the branch's landline phone was passed over to me so I could confirm my availability for overtime after I didn't reply on my personal mobile. As I expected, this grew into a bit of a telling-off that created some tension between me and the company.

"Keep your phone on, yeah?" the area manager said. "All you've got to do is look at your texts... I don't care if you're on a desert island in the middle of nowhere and you've got no signal, don't text me twenty minutes before a shift starts saying you can't come in. If you don't reply, then I'll get someone else." It all sounded like he was talking to a child. I failed to get a word in edgeways. Any explanation I tried to offer hit a brick wall. I was merely trying to clear up my lack of reply as I was on the brink of a panic attack in my new job. *Please could they take me off their 'send to all'?* I was down for the rest of the day, feeling totally useless not long after thinking that I finally fitted into an occupational role. I approached this manager face-to-face in my free time but it didn't help me please the modern mobile mentality. The management quickly lost trust in me over the matter, however human I tried to make my interaction with them. There were several occasions when I was blamed for miscounts in the store, an aspect of the job entirely irrelevant to digital convention. I wasn't responsible each of the times but the lack of trust after my ill-communication via-text seemed to cloud a bigger judgement of me as an employee. *Did they think I was stupid?* If they did, it could only be because I didn't answer my phone. If they could see that I'd made the extra effort to communicate outside of that form, it didn't change their demeanour from suggesting that the job was going to be sub-par from me. I had to bite my lip because I needed the work. Well, I assumed now that it was always extra work to fill a role in a world online. My issue threatened a doctrine of being qualified for anything by the sounds of it. I was on the back foot before I could rise above my frustration and process the outcomes of my heavy disadvantage.

7:8

I woke up one Monday morning in a foul mood as I headed to receive a Covid-19 booster jab. Half-asleep still, I was asked at the door to show a text or email confirmation. When I replied that I didn't have it, there was a roll of the eye as the staff member backed inside to grab a pen and paper for me to prove my date of birth. I then got asked twice more by layers of staff.

After that, "Do you have the NHS app?"

"I don't," I replied flatly.

"If you download it then you can have all your previous vaccination dates." I nodded and thanked the nurse, thinking about the number of times I'd been in a professional service environment where this sort of advice had come up. It was second nature to the staff. I tried my best to remain confident and honest, but it was clear that I was disrupting their well-oiled machine of providing the best possible service. If I ever got caught off guard, wherever I was, I could get a pang of irritation at the assumption that I had these online functions to make things easier, or else I'd interpret a look as implying I was totally ignorant. The angst around it sometimes made my blood boil. I'd spent my whole life uncomfortably moving between online predominance, scarcely believing that I was taking up the physical space that my body filled. No one chose to be allergic to peanuts.

The next day, I woke up early, drenched in a cold sweat. I'd had no side effects beyond a sore arm after my first two jabs, but to my astonishment, this one had wiped me out. I passed out in a friend's bedroom where I was lodging, waking up half an hour after I was supposed to start work. Swearing and leaping out of bed to put any clothes on that I could find, I pushed my lethargic body onto a skateboard outside the door, racing to work with an intense flu and a blazing throat.

"I am so sorry I'm late," I pleaded to my manager, who had had to take her lunch later than expected due to my absent cover.

"What happened?" she asked. I was so tired and weak, but I didn't have time to dwell on whether I should be there. I tried explaining that I felt ill from my booster and overslept, but this didn't seem to suffice.

"Okay..." Here it comes. "I tried calling you and spoke to your mum. I need to have a way of contacting you otherwise you will lose your job." All I could do was stand in front of her and admit my errors.

"Like, if you'd contacted me, it would have been different, but I'm going to have to give you a verbal warning. The next time, it will be a written one, and then after that, you'll lose your job," she said firmly. "Out of work, you can do whatever you want, that's nothing to do with the company. But you need to be contactable directly; it doesn't matter how." I didn't have the energy to even think about arguing with that last part. I felt so rough, nodding my head and then apologizing to my other two colleagues in the store. One of them was just as late the day before after sleeping through his alarm. He phoned in so there was no verbal warning given to him. It took one morning of lost vigilance for me to pay for being uncontactable directly. For the rest of the day my manager barely looked me in the eye. In another world we would have been friends – she was the same age as me and had similar experiences at Sussex uni, but there was one pivot that transformed our relation into an atmosphere of tension. I was an outlaw, and without any of the romantic stuff. My head was down, beanie and face mask on, trying to focus on straightening clothes, so far in the shadows that I ruled out the possibility of asking to go home because of the overwhelming vaccination effects.

7:9

After strictly instructing Mum to hold off reading any of my texts again, I could see her reluctance in granting it, as she reminded me knowingly that I needed to see my friends. I couldn't vanish again. If I dissociated again with the people in my life, I didn't think I'd be able to take it when the shadow reawakened itself to make me collapse into the all-too-familiar vortex of nothingness. No matter, my friend texted Mum on a Friday evening soon after that very conversation. I'd recently phoned Mum on this friend's phone so she took the digital path back round the other way to reach me. As I was about to pack it in for an early night, Mum called up the stairs to pass the message on.

"You just can't get away from it, can you?" she laughed. I proceeded to go out to the pub and meet my friends. Normal ends, peculiar means. I couldn't complain about the ways this constant barrier could be bypassed by good intentions. Even I couldn't predict how this would all play out. At one point, Mum confiscated my phone after we had an argument about the extent of my exposure.

"Fine! Cancel the contract then," I whined, "If I'm not going anywhere with it then get rid of it." Her reaction to my backward steps in addressing the age-old problem made me turn the emotional wind of my frustration.

"Give it back to me! Give me back my phone!" I snarled, barely believing that a twenty-three-year-old could get into this kind of argument with their mum.

"No, I'm going to drop it at Grandma's when I see her tomorrow," she concluded. This was a different level of defeat, a full destabilization that made me lose all ideas of what my relations were with anyone. The subject of a domestic fallout, a ghastly taste of neurosis, and a friendship circle that I felt slipping between my fingers all toppled me over before I could repair all the damage that couldn't be understood by anyone, including myself. Mum ordered me to ask my therapist if there was a support network available, an organizational body who provided social care directly to people with my kind of issue. I knew the answer to that one already, but I obeyed the request.

"The short answer to that is 'no'," the therapist answered frankly. If there was, it was put together electronically so that outreaching clients could only receive help in that way. There was nothing now that I knew how to influence. What I did, whom I saw; it was out of my hands, and there was a searing pain from the thought that no matter how hard I tried, it was all the same underneath. I knocked on my friend's door and entered a small gathering before everyone went off to stay with their folks over the Christmas period. I felt inadequate the moment I joined them, with a strange delusion that I was a task for everyone to have to deal with while they tried to have fun with their lives. All postal addresses had received a handwritten Christmas card from me, another attempt to reconfigure emotional solidarity with everyone's normality. When I got home in the evening after regrettably having had a few drinks, I quietly climbed straight to the room where it had all begun. This was the deepest and most real pain I'd ever known, and I didn't think it was seen by anyone. The extent of it, the obstruction of it, the self-distracting intensity of it, all felt unidentifiable. I failed to show anyone. I couldn't communicate my anguish enough for me to receive the help that I needed, simply to feel safe and fine. I dug into my stationery box and found my penknife, the same one I'd handed to Mum when I was quarantining in my old student house. I flicked open the same blade from it that I remembered accidentally gushing blood from my thumb when I'd first wielded

229

it years before. Fully aware of how sharp it was, I looked at it and thought that I didn't want to hurt myself, but then I also couldn't hack the feelings that had nowhere else to ventilate out my body. There was nothing left that could lessen the burden on my mind. I gripped the knife hard and sliced it down my forearm in a forceful motion.

"Let me bleed it out, if nothing else can take the pain away."

It's Nowhere Near the End

8:1

"How many people do you do that for?" I asked my doctor, as I watched him scrounge for a pen and paper to note a reminder for my next appointment.

He smiled, "Most people put it on their smartphone."

"Do you have anything?" my friend asked. I needed to go home and grab my wallet, but I promised I'd return to meet her at a bar.

"What? Like a phone?" I answered.

"Yeah," she said blankly.

"Like, I get it, it's cool, but in the modern world... like if I was to leave the house and not have my phone, then I couldn't text if I was going to be late to meet someone."

"Do you have Instagram?" someone I met in a bar asked.

"No."

"What's your number then?"

I looked at her with a pause.

"It's okay, you don't have to give it to me," she said, awkwardly.

"No, no, it's not like that. I don't use a phone."

She sighed, "You're one of them."

"You know someone else who's like that?"

"No," she admitted.

"I was gonna say: I'd like to meet them if you did."

"You're not allowed to do that!"

"What?" I replied confusedly.

"Watch a show on Netflix – you don't do those things."

My friend posted in a big group chat, "How is he going to come to London if he doesn't have a phone?" I managed to reunite with another whom I hadn't seen for two years.

"Is there anything you do have? Like a game account or something?" he asked, in front of two others. The tone was friendly, but I was all too familiar with the verbal jousting match, as they'd look to win in front of the group.

My usual weapon of choice was self-mockery, "Didn't you receive my invite on Club Penguin?" He laughed and the conversation moved on.

I told Mum what happened the day after I tried to cut myself. I brought it up myself at the dinner table, when my phone came up in conversation. Mum and my sister gasped. The knife was blunt and had bounced harmlessly off my skin after my stab. I woke up with it on the floor beside my bed, opened out, but I was safe.

My eyes welled up as I spoke about it. "I don't understand how this object could cause so much harm. I can't do anything without it, but I just can't use it normally. Like, why can't I just use it as it should be?" I picked up my sister's smartphone and clasped it with a level of simplicity so different from the scale of the issue surrounding it. Mum looked so hurt.

"How can there be nothing to get you past this? Why can't people make reasonable adjustments? There has to be some kind of support available to get you through this. You're not the only one dealing with all of this. Loads of people aren't well because of it. Something needs to be done." I was still determined to work this out. So many good things had happened for me, yet the very core of where my issues melted out into a solid barrier left me motionless at times. The expectations and the standards of organizing people were out of my reach. Mum told me that all of this didn't have to be considered when she was a teenager. It wasn't a part of the social fabric around her. There was no maturity needed to use it safely, no rash caused if you were unlucky. These modern forms had a huge generational factor in their consumption, but whether you were eight years old or eighty, there were things about connectivity that were difficult to control. If you had the hardware, you could do it all, and no one could really stop you if you were to trip and fall on a part that could be harmful to you. I'd fallen pretty hard from tripping over and the objects changed dramatically ever since but it still affects my life despite having taken myself away from the race, saddened that there are some results afterward that I couldn't obtain like everybody else.

But I know by now that I'm not alone. Well, no. I understand why I haven't yet met anyone in the exact same position as me. But I'm there though for the people who don't always feel good about online life. I'll talk to friends, strangers, human beings, and I'll show my support for them in getting through. I'll ask them questions about cyber-wellbeing if I sense there's something left unsaid. I'll cheer them on if they battle through an uncomfortable little thing in their online world that can contribute to a bigger woe. That big feeling that comes back in ways that are often unexpected; it grows or rests according to its triggers. I want this to be spoken about so that people can connect over it. That's how I've connected better with people, and I didn't even have to revert to my socials. I befriended the managers at that clothes store. The people who'd alienated me for the first year at uni now call me a lifelong friend. I can go out in public without worrying about who might see me, ready to interact with anyone when it happens so that I never feel truly disconnected anymore. The experience that threatened my life is now very different from the past. Life's tough, but I smile when I think about how far I've come to reach a better place, even if I am swimming against the current.

Milton Keynes UK
Ingram Content Group UK Ltd.
UKHW030158010324
438680UK00001B/15